MORE PRAISE FOR "THE CLASSROOM IS BARE"!

"The Classroom is Bare has a powerful message for teachers, for elected officials and for the public. We must set high standards and hold our schools accountable; but without the teacher, the classroom is indeed bare. Linda Favero's story is an inspirational read for all of us."

—Bob Holden
Governor of Missouri

"Lessons of life are taught both inside and outside of the classroom. Linda Favero was a master teacher in both arenas — in spite of and because of her battle with brain cancer. *The Classroom is Bare* is incredible testimony to a remarkable young teacher who touched the lives of both her colleagues and her students!"

—Jere Hochman
Superintendent, Parkway School District
Chesterfield, Missouri

"The Classroom is Bare...the teacher's not there: Labor of love does not begin to describe Martha Karlovetz's book about her daughter, Linda Favero. Linda, who followed her mother into the teaching profession, died of brain cancer two years ago, just days before her 33rd birthday. The title of the book comes from a poem written by a student. The book is a tribute to a remarkable teacher, and reminds us that in a very real way, teachers who love teaching live forever."

—Bill McClellan
St. Louis Post-Dispatch
St. Louis, Missouri

"Teachers who care about kids — all kids — are the key to student learning. Linda Favero was such a teacher as evidenced by the sometimes thoughtful, sometimes humorous notes from her students. Her story, beautifully and poignantly written by her mother, a caring teacher herself, is an inspirational story for all and a "must read" for all who care about what happens in our schools."

—**Don Senti**,*Superintendent,*
School District of Clayton
Clayton, Missouri

"This poignant tale is the mother/daughter *Love Story* of the 21st century. As a courageous team they carefully explore all the options and employ many on the way towards finding the magic bullet—effective brain tumor treatment. It exists for some, but not for all. This love story is a stark reminder of the need for more research and faster progress."

—**Naomi L. Berkowitz**, *Executive Director*
American Brain Tumor Association

The Classroom is Bare is an inspirational story at work on many levels. It tells the story of a committed and talented teacher, Linda Favero. It also tells of Linda's vigorous battle with cancer. At another level, this is a story of a family's journey and the love that carries them through the raw and the good moments. Finally, this is a testimony to the impact classroom teachers have on the lives of their students. At each level, this book is a touching, heart-rending read."

—**Reverend Carl Schenck**, *Senior Pastor*
Manchester United Methodist Church
Manchester, MO

"Every teacher wants to be remembered for the learning instilled, the kindness shared, the courage modeled, and the support and comfort provided to students, parents and peers. Linda Favero was such a teacher. Her love for life and learning is beautifully portrayed in *The Classroom is Bare.*"

—**Chris Guinther**
Missouri NEA Vice President
Member, Board of Directors,
National Board for Professional Teaching Standards

"A teacher never knows how many lives she will touch....this book brings that message home in a riveting, personal way. At the same time, the story of the courage and struggle for two teachers to help each other through the most challenging of times should be an inspiration to us all. While the classroom may be bare, the spirit and courage of this teacher will live on through her students."

—**Kathe Rasch,**
Dean School of Education,
Maryville University, St. Louis, MO

"*The Classroom is Bare* is the moving and inspiring story of a young teacher's promising life and career cut short by brain cancer. Through her courage and perseverance in the face of incredible odds, Linda leaves an enduring legacy, not only for her fifth grade students and their families, but also for the doctors, nurses and other adults who knew her, and for all who read her story."

—**Carol K. Schmoock**
MNEA Assistant Executive Director
For Instruction and Professional Development
Jefferson City, MO

"Linda Favero was a patient who stood out from the crowd, and helped me to see that strength and determination can accomplish remarkable outcomes. She faced seemingly insurmountable obstacles with a determination seldom seen in youth. I was privileged to know her and to participate in a small part of her heroic struggle after being diagnosed with a malignant brain tumor. *The Classroom is Bare* is beautifully written and grants us rare insight into the bond formed between a mother and child during a time of grief. Linda was a remarkable woman whose memories will endure."

—**David Butler, MD**
Radiation Oncology
St. Luke's Hospital, Chesterfield, MO

"A poignant and moving story that will inspire teachers and anyone who has been touched by cancer."

—**Pat Donat**, *author,*
Chalk Dust, Red Tape and Miracles

"A true labor of love as a mother shares her courageous daughter's legacy and the family's journey with brain cancer. Notes from students and parents add an extra dimension to an inspirational story."

—**Father James Sheehan**, *author,*
The Father Who Didn't Know My Name

"The teachers whom we most remember for impacting our lives are those who share their lives as an extension of their curriculum. Linda Favero did just that, and her story is an inspiration to anyone who desires to impact the lives of those around them."

—**Rev. Amy Gearhart Sage**
Senior Pastor, New Hope United Methodist Church
Arnold, MO

"The Classroom is Bare is a wonderful legacy to Linda Favero, a person who taught lessons in her classroom and to all who knew her about courage and determination. This book about her life, triumphs and struggles will help others to appreciate every day and to live each day to its fullest."

—**William E. Rosenfeld**, M.D.,Director
The Comprehensive Epilepsy Care Center for Children and Adults
St. Luke's Hospital, Chesterfield, MO
Board Certified – American Board of Neurology and Psychiatry
Board Certified – American Board of Neurophysiology

"A powerful and compelling story that beautifully illustrates the difference teachers make in the classroom."

—**Reg Weaver**, *President*
National Education Association (NEA)

Dear Candace —

Cherish each moment!

The Classroom is Bare
. . . the teacher's not there

by Martha Karlovetz

Martha Karlovetz

Linmar Publications
www.classroomisbare.com

The Classroom is Bare . . .the teacher's not there
by Martha Karlovetz

For further information, contact the author at:
Linmar Publications
PO Box 1222
Lake Sherwood, MO 63357
(636) 398-5909 • Fax: (636) 398-5909 • Email:
LinmarPub@aol.com
www.classroomisbare.com

Book designed by:
The Floating Gallery
244 Madison Avenue, #254 • New York, NY 10016
(877)822-2500 • www.thefloatinggallery.com

The Classroom is Bare . . .the teacher's not there
Martha Karlovetz

1. Biography—Favero, Linda 2. Teachers—teaching
3. Cancer—brain 4. Bereavement—death of a child

Library of Congress Control Number 2003106869
ISBN 0-9741119-0-2

This book is dedicated to my daughter,
Linda Rebecca Karlovetz Favero,
and to teachers everywhere.

Acknowledgements

THIS BOOK WOULD NOT HAVE been possible without the support of family and friends.

To my husband – and Linda's dad – for the continuous love and support through thirty-eight years of marriage that have helped make so many of my endeavors possible.

To my parents for instilling tenacity, responsibility and a love of life-long learning.

To my brother, Dave, career writer and friend, for his support during Linda's illness and for his encouragement and editing help with this project.

To my brother, Anthony, as he begins his personal fight against cancer.

To Sandy, fellow writer and confidant, for her helpful critiques and practical suggestions.

To Frances for her gracious proofreading assistance.

To all the friends, colleagues, parents and students who offered their assistance and their prayers throughout Linda's illness.

To Dave, Linda's husband, for the beautiful love he shared with our daughter and the courage and strength to carry on.

To Jared, our miracle grandson, for wonderful hugs.

And to Linda, for her love and her inspiration.

Table of Contents

Preface

LINDA AND I TALKED ABOUT writing this book – together. We believed we had a story to tell about teachers and the impact they have on children's lives. Unlike many teachers who may receive an occasional note of gratitude, she had received hundreds of messages from students and parents and former students, wishing her well and saying how much a part of their lives she had been. The response was exceptional because she was hospitalized, recovering from brain surgery, when she was named Teacher of the Year for her school, Mason Ridge Elementary School in the Parkway School District in St. Louis County, Missouri.

Linda lost her seven year battle with brain cancer in August 2001 but not before inspiring teachers, students, parents, friends and family with her grit and determination, her courage and her love of life.

Although Linda couldn't share in the task of writing this book directly, in some ways she did participate in the process – through letters from students and parents and through her completed application for district finalist for Teacher of the Year. She also helped in the writing process by providing the vivid memories and images I have of her, my only daughter, my only child. She would understand that it was impossible to mention everyone that came to visit or help in some way, or wrote a note or said a prayer, and still keep the continuity of the story. She would also remember and be quick to point out someone whom I may have omitted, someone who really should have been mentioned. I hope she will forgive me and I hope they will, too.

But I must caution the reader. Each of us views the events of our lives through a different window on the world, a personal perspective that shapes what we observe and remember. Although this is Linda's story, it is told from my perspective as her mother. Others who were with her during the peaks and valleys of her life's journey will have other memories and other stories to tell, shaped by their own special vantage point and their personal relationship with Linda.

I believe that those of us who were lucky enough to share in her too short life will agree that we were privileged to know and love this courageous young woman, this master teacher.

Chapter One

Diagnosis Times Three

January 8, 2001

I WILL NEVER FORGET THAT bitter cold January morning. We'd gotten up early in order to be at the hospital by the requested 5:30 a.m. It really didn't matter. None of us had slept much the night before. We got ready in silence, each of us with our own thoughts and concerns. The silence continued as we drove on the still deserted highway to the hospital, parked in the garage and entered the big double doors of St. Luke's. The rest of the journey was about to begin.

September 24, 1994

WE HAD TRAVELED to Ohio for cousin Sharon's wedding. At the reception, Linda and I stood at one side of the dance floor, watching the dancing. We were reminiscing about her own beautiful wedding. She teased me about being a "grandma-want-to-be" and then confided that she and Dave were planning to start a family. They had been married for over two years and had recently moved into a new home. Both she and Dave were now established in their jobs – she as a teacher, he as a manager for a manufacturing company. The time was right.

Later that same night Lamar and I awoke in the hotel to the sound of Dave frantically shouting, "Linda! Linda! What's wrong?" and then desparate pounding on the door of our adjoining room. Something was terribly wrong.

We rushed in to find Linda, lying rigid, eyes not seeing but wide open, her face distorted. Later we would learn this was a grand mal seizure. It lasted only five minutes or so but long enough to scare us all. By the time the paramedics arrived, she was conscious again. They assured us that she would be all right for the rest of the night but advised that she see her doctor when she got home to St. Louis.

The next morning it was as if the seizure had never happened. We went to a local pancake restaurant for breakfast. Linda felt fine. We joked about the fact that Lamar had mistakenly put on my slacks in his rush to get dressed before the paramedics arrived – and they almost fit. We chuckled softly and were as amused as the other customers in the restaurant as a man came out of the restroom with the toilet paper trailing behind him. We talked very little about the night before. Somehow it just didn't seem to be that big of a concern in the morning light.

But Linda did see our family physician the next day. She was promptly referred to a neurologist who was quick to diagnose a brain tumor. In a visit to Linda's hospital room he warned, "Forget about teaching and forget about having a family!" He then scheduled an MRI (magnetic resonance image) just to make sure.

The devastating news stunned us all but it also explained some things. This was why Linda had been experiencing headaches for the past few years – headaches resistant to any kind of painkiller. This, too, was why her handwriting had slowed down to the point that it was a struggle for her even to sign her name. She had scheduled an appointment with an orthopedic doctor, thinking she had carpal tunnel syndrome. She had also had some "fainting" spells, but had told no one about them because she wasn't really sure that they had happened.

Three days later the capable and kind Dr. Mendelsohn, a neurosurgeon, confirmed what the neurologist had suspected. "Yes, you have a low grade glioma." He went on to explain that the tumor was about five centimeters in diameter. Its full scientific name was oliodendroglioma. That was the good news, he said, for this kind of tumor is very slow growing.

Unfortunately, the bad news was that the tumor was located directly on the motor strip that controls all movement on the right side of the body. Surgery was out of the question. One infinitesimal slip of the knife and she could be paralyzed for life. Radiation was the best course of action.

Linda asked about the neurologist's prediction that she couldn't go back to teaching. "Hogwash," was Dr. Mendolsohn's strong implication if not exactly a direct quote. "I see no reason why you shouldn't be able to teach once the radiation therapy is completed. But let's not worry about that now."

"What about having children?"

"We'll just have to wait and see. Pregnancy makes everything in your body grow – including tumors. If you were to become pregnant and the tumor should grow, then we would have two problems."

And so we waited for more tests and to see another doctor. Medical students kept stopping by to visit. Each time Linda would obligingly close her eyes and raise her arms. Each time the students would watch as her right arm dropped involuntarily. They'd wish her well and go on to another patient. But a couple of them kept coming back. They'd ask me in the hall, "How's she doing? How's she taking this?"

"Just fine," was my reply.

At this point, we were all still totally optimistic and totally naïve. OK, so she had a tumor but it was just a low-grade glioma, after all. It was going to be treated with radiation and then she could get on with her life.

Friday afternoon we gathered in Linda's room, waiting to meet with the radiation oncologist. Rachel, Dave's mom, had driven in from Lockport, Illinois. Jan, a long-time friend of Linda's and mine, had come to visit Linda and meet me. We planned to head to Jefferson City for a meeting as soon as we met with the doctor. At least that was the plan.

When Dr. Butler finally entered the room it was nearly 4:00 p.m. He was younger than Dr. Mendohlson, very good looking and very professional. He introduced himself and then said, "Usually when we treat this form of cancer, we. . ."

We hardly heard anything else he said. We'd heard about gliomas all week but this was the first time we'd heard the word, "*Cancer*!" I suspect that this was just the first time it really registered. This wasn't just a brain tumor. This was *Cancer*. That's why those medical students had been so concerned. That's why they kept stopping by and asking how she was doing. They were about the same age as Linda. They realized this could have been one of them!

Linda started radiation treatments the following Monday. She was to have thirty treatments in all, the maximum dose she could take, five days each week for six weeks. On weekends her sunburned-looking scalp would be given a rest. She took a medical leave of absence from teaching. Parents and teachers arranged to drive her to St. Luke's for the treatments, as she couldn't drive for at least six months following the seizure.

The first step in the treatment was to make a custom-fitted, Darth Vader-like mask to hold her head completely rigid so the radiation could be sent directly to its target. She faced the treatments bravely, using each session to will the cancer from her body, and keeping the optimism that was going to give her the strength to combat the disease and inspire everyone she met.

In February, Linda returned to her sixth grade classroom at Pierremont Elementary School. As she would be throughout her illness, she was frank and open with both her students and their parents. Yes, she had cancer, but that wasn't the end of the world. Her scalp was still too burned to wear a wig, so she wore hats to cover the large spot on her head where hair would never grow again. One of her students, with full parental permission, shaved his head in a show of support. As she walked down the hall one day, a second grader whispered to her, "Mrs. Favero, we aren't supposed to wear hats in school."

"I know," she said, "but I have special permission from the principal."

LINDA HAD GROWN up with the goal of becoming a teacher. As a little girl she had been my "guinea pig" as I learned how to give diagnostic reading and intelligence tests. She would help me make games and cut out award charts for use in my reading classes. In high school she was a sixth grade camp counselor. During her last two summers in high school she had worked as a student aide in a summer "essentials" program, a program to give younger students an extra boost in reading and math that I had helped plan and supervised. She was wonderful with kids in the school setting and in our neighborhood where she was in great demand as a babysitter.

I worried at times that she wanted to be a teacher just because I was a teacher. School had not been easy for Linda. In elementary school she struggled some both with reading and math – and talking too much. In junior high she would be fine when she went to school but would frequently get legitimate tummy aches once she was there and I would get the call to take her home. These headaches were ultimately diagnosed as being caused by psychosomatic depression, treatable and curable but doing little to bolster her self-confidence.

Linda was on the fringes of the activity in school, being neither especially academically or athletically talented – just a nice, average student trying to find her special niche. The August before she was to enter ninth grade she faithfully attended intramural volleyball practice every day only to be cut from the team just before school started. That's when Lamar and I surprised her on her birthday with horseback riding lessons at a stable across the street from the school.

That same year she began to get active in our church youth group and the youth choir. These activities helped fill the social and emotional gap that school did not provide. The church youth activities also provided a safe culture where drugs and alcohol weren't "the thing" to do.

Linda continued to struggle academically and really had to study to maintain a "B" average. From my perspective, one of the reasons she had difficulty in school was because she spent so much time beautifully organizing her materials, making charts and setting up elaborate notebooks, that she sometimes didn't reserve enough time to actually study. I smile when I think how these same organizational skills were to prove very beneficial to her later as a teacher.

Her activities at church and her junior year of high school helped turn the tide. Parkway West had an "Academic

Decathlon Team" that competed with other area high schools. The team consisted of two "Honors" students, two "A" students and one or two "B" students. Linda was named one of the "B" students on the team, putting her in contact with some excellent role models for developing good study skills. Linda added some balance and common sense to the team – and thrived in that position.

Even so, when senior prom time arrived, Linda was one of the girls who didn't have a date. That didn't stop her. She had a friend fix her up with a blind date, a young man who was going to be home from college, and on the day of the prom bought the dress, the shoes – the works.

Linda chose Illinois Wesleyan University in Lockport, Illinois, a small university with an excellent reputation. She had the typical freshman year struggle – and continued to find Spanish a curse – but would later tease her dad and me that she did finish in four years. In college, she blossomed, joining Kappa Kappa Gamma sorority and meeting Dave, the love of her life, who just happened to bus tables at the sorority house.

Linda's commitment to teaching never wavered. Perhaps her own struggles through school contributed to this motivation and led to her later strength as a teacher. She knew what it was like not to be the "superstar" in class–she had lived it! When she graduated from Illinois Wesleyan in 1990 with an elementary teaching degree, teaching jobs were scarce. The Parkway School District in the western St. Louis County suburbs was her district of choice. Linda was a product of Parkway, having attended school there from kindergarten through high school graduation. I had been a teacher there as well. The district has an excellent reputation and could afford to be choosy when selecting teachers; only rarely did they hire beginning teachers.

Opting to get some experience under her belt, Linda taught her first year in Harvey, Illinois, a small urban school district with all the challenges these districts face: poverty, drugs, limited resources. She was teaching, however, doing what she had been trained for and always wanted to do. Harvey was closer to Dave, too, who was completing his senior year at Illinois Wesleyan. In fact, Linda lived with Dave's family that year, giving them an opportunity to really get to know her and to become close.

After graduation, Dave got a job with a small manufacturing company based in Chesterfield, Missouri, so Linda moved back home. She signed up to substitute in Parkway and worked in a gift store while she waited to be called. By January, she was subbing almost every day, broadening her experience at every elementary grade. She taught summer school and then, shortly before school started, landed a spot teaching second grade at River Bend.

Even so, as the new teacher on the block, the following year she was transferred to another school, Pierremont, and a sixth grade position. While she loved teaching at Pierremont and they loved her, she readily accepted a transfer to a more permanent fifth-grade position at Mason Ridge. She was open and up front about her cancer from the first day. Each year, and sometimes over her principal's objections, she introduced herself to parents with a letter. She told them she had cancer but assured them that her illness would not interfere with their children's education. Although some parents had qualms at first, these vanished quickly and they became her strongest allies. Notes from parents confirm that support and also illustrate Linda's practice of treating parents as equal partners – on a first-name basis.

Dear Linda,
Thank you for your very candid and uplifting letter! I am thrilled that Jay is in your class this year, and

your letter reinforced what I had already anticipated –
he will learn a great deal from someone with your
amazing spirit and outlook.

I look forward to working with you this year and
genuinely hope you will let me know how I may be of
assistance. I would be happy to help in any way.

Best wishes, Suzanne

Dear Linda ,

Enclosed is Robert's poppy journal assignment.
Thank you for giving him an extension for completion.
Gary and I greatly appreciated the opportunity to meet
with you on Friday. We commend you for creating such
an excellent learning environment that encourages
respect, disciplined learning and self-responsibility
with a focus on the future.

Thanks again, Maureen

LINDA WAS ALSO honest and up front with her students. She told
them about her illness, the treatments she had had, and
answered their questions. She even brought her MRI scans and
her Darth Vader mask to the classroom. And, once each year,
she took off her wig to help take the mystery out of what was
underneath. She accepted always having to wear a hat or a
wig as nonchalantly as she accepted everything else about her
disease. It was simply a fact of life. She kept a ball cap on a
hook by the front door, primarily so she wouldn't startle
someone rather than from any sort of embarrassment. And she
replaced her synthetic but authentic-looking wigs each year.
As she would say, she never had to worry about having a "bad-
hair day."

Fall 1995

IRONICALLY, MASON RIDGE was also the school where I had been
the reading specialist for two years. I taught there prior to
taking a leave of absence to serve nine years as president of
the Missouri National Education Association (MNEA), a tenure
that ended in August of 1995. Although I could have returned
to Parkway, I chose instead to take advantage of an early-
retirement incentive offered that year. Under this agreement I

was to work in the district at least one day each school year for seven years so that I could still be considered an "employee" and eligible for pay.

These "work" days I chose to do in Linda's classroom, with both her blessing and the blessing of the principal. Most of these early-retirement days I helped provide an extra hand for field trips or gave presentations about places where Lamar and I had traveled. Thus I knew quite a bit about her classes and also had had a chance to observe, first-hand, what a wonderful teacher she was. We could never repeat the surprise we gave Linda's students my first work day as a retiree.

Linda was young and a new teacher in the building. She was a good disciplinarian but also had a very relaxed, easy way in her classroom. That first year at Mason Ridge she joked that sometimes she thought the kids took advantage of her easy manner and she was going to have to crack down more. That reminded me of a favorite children's book I had used when I was teaching: *Miss Nelson is Missing* by Bernard Waber. The premise of the book is that a young teacher finds her students getting out of control so comes to school dressed in a wicked-looking disguise as the mean substitute, Viola Swamp. After a day of experiencing Viola Swamp, the kids are more than happy to behave with Miss Nelson.

Linda and I decided that I would go to Mason Ridge as Viola Swamp. We planned the appearance to the minute detail. Linda always took photos of each child at the beginning of the school year. We used these photos so that I could learn the names of her students – sight unseen – and know a little bit about each of them. I wore one of Linda's wigs and a black sweatshirt imprinted "Viola Swamp." It was the day of Halloween parties anyway, so coming in "costume" was not unusual.

Linda was sequestered in the closet at the back of her classroom, as I greeted each child as they came into the room, calling them by name and introducing myself as Mrs. Swamp. We even had Mr. Ramsey, the principal, involved. He stopped by to chat with Mrs. Swamp and make sure everything was going smoothly. But the kids knew something wasn't quite right. One boy, looking me straight in the eye, said, "You look a lot like Mrs. Favero but a lot older." I turned quickly to hide my chuckle.

Shortly before the first bell rang, one of the kids figured out who I was and even remembered my name. "Mrs. Karlovetz?" he called and I instinctively turned around. With that Linda came out from her hiding place in the closet and our joke was over. Yet, she had gotten her point across and some of those students still remember that day. (I spent the rest of the day as Viola Swamp reading *Miss Nelson is Missing* to primary children.)

WITH LINDA TAKING the lead, life got back to normal, or so it seemed. We put our fears aside and went on as we waited. Each time the appointment for the next MRI drew near, we all got a little nervous again although we wouldn't have admitted it to each other. Sometimes Linda didn't even tell us ahead of time that an appointment had been made so that we wouldn't worry. For each MRI, she worked out a plan – first the MRI, then a visit with Dr. Butler, the oncologist, then a trip to Dr. Mendelsohn's office. She'd carry her MRI scans with her most of the time, often stopping in the stairway to peek. By this time, we were beginning to feel like novice MRI interpreters. When the news was good, we'd head to a nearby local restaurant and indulge in a wonderful lunch, complete with its famous homemade pie.

This became our routine.

One year after the initial diagnosis, an MRI finally confirmed that the tumor had shrunk from five centimeters to two-and-a-half. "That might be all the radiation will do," the doctors said. "We'll just have to wait and see."

It was difficult to tell from the MRIs whether what remained was scar tissue or tumor. If it was scar tissue, OK. But if it was tumor, it could always begin to grow again. Linda would probably have MRIs every four to six months for the rest of her life just to make sure.

Following each MRI, Linda would ask her doctors, "What about having children?"

May 1996

FOUR MRIS AFTER THE initial diagnosis and eighteen months later, the doctors finally said, "OK, the tumor seems to be stable. Go ahead!"

I learned the results of this latest MRI through a very special Mother's Day card. The printed message said, "Happy Mother's Day from your little girl," but Linda had added:

Dear Mom –

Happy Mother's Day is not enough to express everything I need to say. Thank you for all of your love, support and friendship. I would not be the person I am today without the guidance you and Daddy gave me. Now that I realize one should never take life, health and happiness for granted, thank you for giving me all of them. Without the love and support of friends and family during the past year-and-a-half, I would not be able to maintain my positive outlook and attitude.

May 10, 1996 – another good report and MRI. Happy Mother's Day!

Love, Linda

June 1996

THE EVENING BEFORE Father's Day, Linda and Dave came to our house for dinner. They presented me with a small bouquet of flowers and a book by Robert Munsch, *Love You Forever*. This beautiful children's book is about the love between mother and child through every stage of life. As a retired reading teacher, I am always interested in children's books but Linda insisted that we sit down and read this one right then.

Inside the front cover she had paraphrased the message of the story and inscribed:

> *Dear Mom and Daddy,*
> *I'll love you forever,*
> *I'll like you for always,*
> *As long as I'm living*
> *My parents you'll be.*
> *Love always, Linda*

Hugs and kisses followed and then Linda insisted again, "Read the story!" And so I read. On the very last page of the book, she had written:

Congratulations! You two are going to be grandparents!

Again, hugs and kisses – and tears – all around. So much for the neurologist's prediction that she should forget about having children!

We were ecstatic about the news. And so were Linda and Dave.

LITTLE DID WE know the frightening hurdles that loomed ahead. The first ultrasound showed everything developing smoothly. At sixteen weeks into her pregnancy, Linda was given some special diagnostic blood tests. These had been ordered partly because of the cancer and radiation therapy. The phone rang shrilly early one morning.

"Mom, how fast can you get to St. Luke's?"

Linda and Dave had received a call early that morning, too. One of the blood tests indicated that there was a possibility that the baby had a chromosome deficiency called Trisomey 13. They had an appointment with a genetics counselor that morning which was to be followed by another ultrasound. I made the thirty-five mile trip to St. Luke's faster than I have ever done before – or since.

The counselor went over all the possibilities and explained what this deficiency meant – the baby lacked a thirteenth chromosome. Most children born with this abnormality did not live past the age of two although a few have lived into adulthood. The purpose of the ultrasound was to check for deformities in the fetus that can occur with this deficiency. If the deficiency existed, there would be some tough decisions to make. The tension that clogged that dimly lit ultrasound room was suffocating. Dave couldn't even bring himself to look. I sat holding Linda's hand while a technician and a specially trained doctor moved the wand over Linda's belly, carefully avoiding the genital area because they didn't want to know the sex of the fetus – especially if anything was wrong.

First they checked for the stomach and feet. Everything appeared to be normal. But there are degrees of this deficiency.

The doctor really needed to see the infant's hands before a definitive conclusion could be made. Hands of a Trisomey 13 fetus would be clenched tight and possibly deformed. But the fetus was asleep and its hands were hidden from view.

We waited.

Finally, the doctor had Linda get up and move around in an effort to wake up the fetus and get it to move; then another try.

The baby appeared to be sleeping still. But then, as we watched in amazement, the fetus shifted slightly and a tiny, perfectly formed little hand came up from behind its back, and waved at us as if to say, "Hi, folks. I'm OK. See you in about five months."

Even the doctor and the technician had tears in their eyes!

As A FIFTH grade teacher, Linda had quickly become involved in the Missouri Drug Abuse Resistance Education (D.A.R.E) program. The D.A.R.E. officer who worked with her was so impressed with Linda's approach that she nominated her for the D.A.R.E. Teacher of the Year Award. Not only was Linda named the Parkway D.A.R.E. Teacher of the Year, she was also selected as the Missouri D.A.R.E. Teacher of the Year for 1996. Dave, Lamar and I were invited to the luncheon for the award-winning teachers from school districts statewide. (We were in on the secret that she was the Missouri D.A.R.E. Teacher but Linda didn't know until it was announced.) In her unanticipated acceptance speech, Linda closed by saying, "One of the things I try to teach my kids is that you can be a cancer survivor. As proof of this," she said proudly, "my husband and I are expecting our first child."

YET ANOTHER HURDLE to cross occurred late in her pregnancy. The baby stopped moving. Another ultrasound was ordered – still being careful not to reveal the sex of the child. Once again, a huge sigh of relief. The ultrasound showed that the baby was all right but had positioned itself feet-first – a Caesarian was in order.

Jared Tyler Favero was born on February 28, 1997.

Kay, a student nurse finishing up her time in obstetrics, had asked Linda if she could be in attendance in the delivery room. Linda readily agreed. Kay, you see, was a Mason Ridge parent but she also understood Linda's situation only too well. Her first-born son had died of a brain tumor.

Dave, of course, was with Linda during the surgery while I waited as patiently as possible down the hall. It was Kay who brought Jared to me while the surgical team was finish-

Linda and Jared, miracle baby, April 1997

ing with Linda. It was Kay who handed me that adorable bundle, the grandchild we thought we would never have.

The newly born Jared was then whisked to the nursery for all the routine things hospitals do with new babies. Shortly thereafter, Linda was wheeled down the hall. As they passed the nursery windows, Linda cried, "Can I see him?" The nurses held up a screaming, 8 pound, 13 ounce, boy. The tears that followed were tears of pure joy—he truly was our miracle baby!

Two years later . . .

AND SO THEY would all live happily ever after – at least we hoped. But it was not to be.

Yes, Jared did grow and thrive and was such a special blessing. Linda returned to Mason Ridge in the spring, just before the end of that school year. She continued to love teaching. She even surprised us by finally finishing her Master's thesis, a project that had been interrupted twice, first with the diagnosis of a tumor, then with the pregnancy. Dave continued to do well and was a devoted company man. Lamar

Linda and Jared making cookies, October 1998

and I quickly became doting grandparents. Dave's parents, Rick and Rachel were, too, but lived five hours away.

The doctors had warned that the MRIs must continue just to make sure that the shady grayish-white spot on the scan didn't start to grow. The first two MRIs following Jared's birth were fine. By the third one, we were almost complacent that things would go well once again. So sure were Linda and Dave, they even brought twenty month-old Jared with them to show off to the radiation oncology staff. From this grandmother's biased eyes, he looked adorable and very grown up, dressed in tan corduroys and a crew neck sweater, running down the long hospital corridor.

Linda had the MRI and we headed to radiation oncology and the appointment with Dr. Butler. We waited. The nurse came in to see how we were doing and brought some toys for Jared. We still waited. Jared was getting restless by now as any two-year-old would. The longer we waited the more apparent it became that something was wrong.

Finally Dr. Butler entered the consultation room. "I have bad news," he said. "The scans show that the tumor may have started to grow."

Stunned silence. Then tears.

Jared came over to his mommy and hugged her knees. "Don't cry, Mommy," he said. "Everything's going to be all right."

And things did continue to be all right. Surgery was still not an option due to the location of the tumor. Linda had already had the maximum dosage of radiation therapy she could have in her lifetime. Chemotherapy is generally the treatment of last resort for brain tumors. Most chemos available today for other forms of cancer can't get past the blood-brain barrier – the same thing that inhibits many chemicals, except for alcohol, from reaching the brain.

Linda was referred to a chemotherapy oncologist, a young woman about her age I know only as Julie. Julie and Linda hit it off instantly and Julie was eager to make her mark on the cutting edge of medicine. Linda quickly became part of a phase II study for Temadol, a new chemotherapy that seemed to offer promise for brain tumor patients and had minimal side effects. One advantage of this kind of chemo is that it is all done through oral medication. The disadvantage for women patients, with this or any chemotherapy, is that you probably should not have children afterwards. Too little is yet known about the long-term side effects of chemo on the eggs that could lead to severe abnormalities.

Linda and Dave would have to settle for one child. But there are worse things. Linda, herself, was an only child. She was just as strong, determined and philosophical as ever. I remember her sharing with me once as we drove to one of the many doctors' appointments, "Mom, we're all going to die sometime. Unlike most people, I know how I'm going to die. I just don't know when."

So the chemo treatment began, five days out of every twenty-eight. Other than being tired and gaining some weight, Linda seemed to be doing very well. As she explained, she had three weeks out of every four to get everything done she wanted to do. Teaching and taking care of a toddler were about all she could accomplish the week she had chemo. In fact, she missed few days in the classroom thanks to a compassionate school nurse – and an understanding principal – who let her lie down in the nurse's office during her late-afternoon planning period.

One MRI came, then another and another. Dr. Butler was reassuring that everything seemed to be on track. Dr. Julie had gone on family leave, but the new chemo-oncologist, Dr. Busick, was also reassuring. He felt, however, that Linda needed to go off the Temadol because she was beginning to have some of the long-term, cumulative side effects. Neither doctor would respond positively to Linda's persistent questions about having another child.

Life went on. Everything was going well.

The Millennium

WE HAD BEEN planning a Millennium vacation for over two years. The impetus was the turn of the century, but Linda's diagnosis had made us much more conscious of making the most of every day. The plans had started with four families but had whittled down to the Bierks, our close friends, and us: seniors, juniors and grandchildren, thirteen people in all. We had had reservations for over two years at Disney World for the Christmas holidays and then on to Sanibel Island, Florida, for New Year's.

Lamar and I had driven to Florida in advance so that we could take "Christmas" with us in our van. The rest of the clan came by plane. The "Tree-top" villas we had booked at Disney World worked perfectly for families, giving us small kitchens and plenty of living area. We had breakfast Christmas Eve morning in the Cinderella Castle and dinner Christmas night at Epcot, complete with Disney characters. At the villas on Christmas Eve we had prime rib and presents and even a (very) small Christmas

Linda and Jared, Disney World, December 1999

tree. Jared, age three, and the Bierk's oldest grandson, Connor, age four, gave us all a chance to enjoy the wonders of Disney from a child's perspective. Jared's favorite ride was Snow White although he called it the "really scary ride."

"Can we go on the really scary ride again?" And we did. Many times.

Bidding Disney goodbye, we headed for two condos we had rented on Sanibel Island. A virus hit many of us during this time and hit Jared the hardest. Still, we each had time to walk the beach and gather shells and were thankful that we were all together.

Summer 2000

EVERYTHING WAS GOING so well that Dave and Linda began thinking about buying a bigger house, one with a better yard for Jared, a better kitchen for Linda who loved to cook and more room for an expanded family.

Linda called me from her cell phone one afternoon. "Mom, can you come?"

She had discovered a new subdivision that was having a grand opening very close to their current home. The homes were in the right price range and had just the floor plan she wanted. A realtor had taken her to another subdivision where she could see an actual display model. Linda was convinced this was the right house for them. Dave was coming after work but she wanted to show me the drawings, too.

To entice prospective buyers, a new marketing gimmick was being tried. This was Friday afternoon. The grand opening would be Saturday at 8:00 a.m. Those who signed up and took a number would be the first people to choose a lot. There was a price incentive, too, as well as a thirty-day escape clause if you changed your mind. The catch was that once you took a number you couldn't leave the site for more than an hour and a half or you would lose your spot. Linda had number seventeen. The couple who would choose first had been camping out for two days. Linda wanted to spend the night in the van and wanted me to stay with her, knowing that Dave and her father would think we were insane.

Dave and Lamar came later in the day to stake out the land and look at the plans. Lot #6 looked like the prime lot, knowing what some of the others ahead of them had already selected. They both agreed the subdivision looked promising. If we were crazy enough to spend the night, that was all right with them as long as they didn't have to.

Linda and I stayed. The builder supplied hot dogs and promotional lights and chairs around a makeshift campfire. Linda met the other young couples waiting, sharing their excitement. We didn't sleep much – there was too much to talk about. At dawn we left for our allotted time off (carefully watched by the others waiting) for a quick shower. We returned with Dave, Jared and Lamar and resumed our place in line. Later that morning, they signed a contract to build a house on Lot #6.

❖ ❖ ❖ ❖

AUGUST CAME AND time for another MRI. This time the news was not simply good. It was fantastic!

"After the next MRI, I think we can go to just once a year," Dr. Butler said. "The calcifications on the tumor appear to be gone!"

Dr. Busick and Dr. Mendelsohn both agreed. We wished Dr. Mendelsohn well, for he would be retired by the time Linda had her next MRI.

We quickly retreated to our favorite fabulous-pie restaurant and continued planning and talking about the new house. That fall Linda and Dave had much fun picking out light fixtures, carpeting and all the things that go

August 22, 2000
Linda's 32nd birthday

into a new house. We shared their joy for they often included us in these expeditions.

Life was beautiful – or so it seemed.

I<small>T WAS A GRADUAL</small> thing. We all noticed it that same fall but none of us said anything to each other. Was Linda relying on her left arm more and more? No, we thought, just compensating so well the way she had always done. She had learned to do almost everything on the computer for her classroom, typing left handed because it was faster. The kids helped by writing on the chalkboard. She even told me once that the kids had held up her right arm when she was trying to staple something high up on a bulletin board. She went to an occupational therapist for awhile but it didn't help much. She did, however, learn to use some compensating devices – such as left-handed scissors and one-handed food-choppers.

My most vivid recollection of the difference is from late October. Linda and Dave were out for the evening. Lamar and I were at the Bierks' home to share grandchild sitting as their home was so much closer than the forty miles away where we lived. When Linda arrived, Jared greeted her eagerly and reached for her to pick him up. I noticed how carefully she bent down to scoop him up, shifting so that his weight would be on her left arm.

"It's only my imagination," I thought, refusing to acknowledge anything more.

So Linda and Dave continued planning for their new house and Lamar and I looked forward to one of those once-in-a-lifetime trips to Peru, Ecuador and the Galapagos Islands. Shortly before we were to leave, Linda told us that she had scheduled an MRI for December 15, after we returned. She wanted to have it behind her before Christmas, she explained. To this day, I think she knew something was wrong but didn't want to spoil our trip.

December 2000

DECEMBER 15 CAME. Dave and I both joined Linda for what we thought would be a routine MRI. I'm not sure Linda thought the same. For one thing, she didn't stop to peek at the scans en route to radiation oncology. Did she suspect something?

We waited and waited for what seemed like an eternity. Once again, Dr. Butler came into the consultation room and said, "I'm afraid I have bad news." This time it was *really* bad. He put up the scans and we could clearly see not one, but two new tumors on either side of the original tumor. They appeared to be about the same size but starkly white – not a good sign on a scan.

"What are the options?" we asked.

"Another form of chemo is probably the only one," he replied, "but I will check with a neurosurgeon."

As we left the radiation oncology area, Dr. Butler pulled Dave aside. "It's bad," he said. "You really need to see if you can get out of your contract for that new house."

Dave shared that information with Lamar and me as we waited for Linda to use the restroom. "Don't tell her that yet," I pleaded.

From there we went to Dr. Busick. He really didn't see surgery as an option. There was just too much risk of permanent paralysis. He thought Linda should get started on chemo right away but wasn't very optimistic about that either.

That night we gathered at Dave and Linda's house for a gloomy dinner and to let the news sink in. As children have a way of doing, Jared knew instinctively that something was wrong. "Mommy," he said. "Why are you crying? Did you go to the doctor's today and did a doctor stick a needle in you?"

"No," Linda replied, "I'm just sad."

DR. BUTLER HAD said he would check with a neurosurgeon regarding the possibility of surgery. Linda at least wanted to hear what he had to say. Dr. Mollman, a surgeon from Dr. Mendolsohn's office, was recommended to us. He and a neurologist, Dr. Rosenfeld, were experienced in doing a special kind of neurosurgery which "mapped" the brain to see just what parts of the brain were controlling which function so that there would be no miscalculations during surgery.

Linda had taken a medical leave from school immediately upon hearing the news. Fortunately, the Parkway School District had a long-standing, unlimited sick leave policy, designed to help in cases of long-term, catastrophic illnesses just like this. She and I set up for a long Christmas baking stint as we waited to hear from Dr. Mollman. We waited and we cooked. In fact, Linda made over sixty loaves of poppy seed bread, one for every member of the staff at Mason Ridge – and all with her left hand! Three days, many loaves of bread and dozens of Christmas cookies later, the call finally came. Dr. Mollman had reviewed the scans and wanted to see her.

Dr. Mollman seemed to be much younger than the venerable and kind Dr. Mendelsohn, but then no neurosurgeons are really young. He was pleasant and straightforward. He put up the scans and said, "Look, you're young and this is an aggressive tumor. I think we have to do something progressive and proactive to deal with this."

"You're my kind of doctor!" Linda quickly agreed.

At any other time of year, Linda's surgery would have been done immediately, but the holiday season would cause a delay. Dr. Rosenfeld was out of town plus a full five-day workweek was needed for this kind of surgery which was actually two surgeries, not just one. On a Monday, they would do a craniotomy, opening her skull to place a band of sixty-four electrodes on the brain. After the swelling had gone down sufficiently, probably in a day or two, Dr. Rosenfeld would do the brain mapping. Finally, on a Friday, Dr. Mollman would do a second surgery, remove the electrodes and remove what tumor they could, based on what had been learned in the mapping. Chemotherapy might still be necessary following the surgery.

The earliest the surgery could be scheduled was January 8. And so we left Dr. Mollman's office to celebrate Christmas.

CHRISTMAS WAS A three-part celebration. On December 21, we had the traditional Bierk/Karlovetz clan party at our home. I have always loved to decorate to the hilt and bake to oblivion for the holidays and this year was no exception.

Both Bierk boys, Todd and Mark, came with their wives and children. These young men were like brothers to Linda. They had grown up together, sharing many good times and a few spankings together. They presented Linda with a beautiful porcelain angel as a symbol of good luck. We wined and dined and unwrapped presents. On the surface it was a joyous occasion, but Linda's pending surgery was the unspoken threat looming in the back of everyone's thoughts.

Linda insisted that she wanted to have this Christmas Eve and Christmas at her home, so that Jared could have the thrill of Santa coming to his own house. Lamar and I arrived in time for our traditional Christmas Eve dinner of *shrimp de johnge*. Jared was allowed to open one present and then put cookies out for Santa. Dave went to Mass.

Linda had converted to Catholicism at the time of her marriage – for all the right reasons. She had since become somewhat disillusioned with the Catholic Church, feeling that the church was not fulfilling her significant spiritual needs as she battled cancer. Manchester Methodist, the church she had attended growing up, was visible along the highway en route to Dave and Linda's home. Lamar and I had not been members of the church since we moved to our lake place some forty miles away. We had lost track of who's who but had watched the progress of the huge addition being built. And Linda and I had made a commitment to go there sometime.

On Christmas Eve we finally went. We marveled over the beautiful, high-tech new sanctuary. The service was beautiful. We were surprised to discover that Amy, a high school youth group and choir-friend, had joined the ministry. It was Amy who had inspired Linda to attend Illinois Wesleyan. Seeing Amy that evening was a coincidence that would prove providential.

Christmas morning we opened presents and shared Jared's excitement about what Santa had brought. Dave had a very special gift for Linda – a pair of diamond earrings. He had had fun planning this gift. Some of the women he worked with teased him about his excellent taste. When Linda opened the gift – and then learned that they were diamonds and not rhinestones – she was speechless. Dave had certainly chosen a wonderful way to let her know that he knew she would be all right.

TWO DAYS LATER Linda and Dave and Jared left for part three of their Christmas, a visit with Dave's family in Illinois. Lamar and I left, too, for Sanibel Island, Florida, where we had rented a condo for the month of January with the Bierks. I had plane reservations to return on January 7, however, to be there for Linda's surgery. I also had reservations to return to Florida a week later when we all presumed she would be out-of-the-woods.

On January 4, Linda and Dave met with Dr. Rosenfeld, who explained the mapping procedure and the risks involved. Linda called us that evening to tell us about the visit. Dr. Rosenfeld was very encouraging and they had liked him immediately. He was open and frank about the risks involved, which included paralysis and loss of speech – or both. Linda was convinced that these were risks she had to take. She reassured me by saying, "Of course, they have to tell you what the risks are but that doesn't mean that anything has to happen."

Why then, as I walked the beautiful Sanibel Beach, did I have this ominous premonition that I was on borrowed time, that I might not be coming back after all? I shared this with Nancy as we walked one morning, finding starfish and enjoying the sound of the waves. She understood and we both prayed silently to ourselves that Linda would be all right.

January 7, 2001

LAMAR AND I were silent as he drove me to the Fort Myers airport for my flight to St. Louis. We were each too absorbed in our own thoughts and fears to be much comfort to the other. As I looked over towards him, I could see the tears on his cheeks, tears that matched my own. He and Linda had an especially close father-daughter relationship. Lamar had worked the "graveyard" shift for Linda's first ten years. He had quickly adjusted to being a twentieth century dad when I returned to work part-time when Linda was one year old and full time when she was three. It was Daddy who generally picked Linda up at pre-school each day. It was Daddy who Linda came home to from morning kindergarten, sliding open our patio door and waking him up. They had spent many wonderful afternoons together and, occasionally, Lamar would even exchange baby-sitting stints with other stay-at-home moms. He was also the one who was home when Linda came home from elementary school, the first parent with whom she could share her day. Linda adored her daddy even though he was often the disciplinarian.

Linda's and my relationship had been more turbulent, especially during those difficult teen years. Fortunately from her vantage point, I was very involved with my local NEA, serving as president during her high school years. This gave us a more peaceful distance. By the time she was in college, I was president of Missouri NEA, the state organization. I remember Linda asking, "Does this mean the teachers at Illinois Wesleyan will know who you are, too?"

"Not likely," I said.

Our relationship improved when she graduated from college and we ultimately became very close friends. I was proud that she had become a teacher. Lamar and I were both pleased that she had chosen Dave to be our son-in-law. And Linda and I had had a wonderful time planning the wedding, waiting in anticipation for Jared – and just this year, planning for the new house.

THE FLIGHT BACK to St. Louis was uneventful. Linda, Dave and Jared met me at the airport. To the casual observer, they could have been any young family picking up grandma for a visit.

On the way to Linda and Dave's home, we stopped at the site of their new house. They were eager to show me the progress that had been made. The second floor and the roof had been completed. Linda was uncertain whether her weakened right side would allow her to successfully negotiate the narrow treads on the makeshift stairway, so Dave, Jared and I went upstairs and gave her a full report. Excited and satisfied that the house was beginning to take shape, we went home to get ready for the next day.

As I unpacked, I noticed a note in the guest room/study where I was staying: "Linda, call Karen A." and then a phone number. I recognized the name immediately. Karen had been my cooperating teacher when I had done my student teaching over thirty years before. We had become friends at the time but lost track of each other as our life pathways diverged.

I went into Linda's room where she was packing. "Linda," I asked, "how do you know Karen?"

"I don't," she answered. Then she explained that a parent from Mason Ridge had given her Karen's name. Apparently her son had also had a brain tumor that had been treated successfully and she had become an advocate for the cause. Karen had called a couple of times when Linda was not at home. Linda hadn't returned the calls because their plan of action had already been determined, but she didn't mind if I called.

Karen hadn't made the connection between Linda and me because of Linda's married name. We caught up on lost time only very briefly and then she asked what the plans were. She expressed concern that we hadn't gotten another opinion. Why didn't we take her to the M.D. Anderson Cancer Center in Texas or to a Dr. Prados in California where her son had been treated?

I'm glad I called and not Linda. Karen meant well but at this point there were no other alternatives. It was five in the afternoon. Surgery was scheduled for the next morning. We'd been the second opinion route when Linda's cancer recurred the first time and were still confident that she was in good hands. It wouldn't do Linda any good to raise doubts at this point.

The die had been cast.

Chapter 2

Surgery

January 8, 2001

AND SO WE ARRIVED AT the hospital on that cold January morning. The automatic doors closed behind us as we walked down the long corridor to "Same Day Surgery." Linda changed into the required hospital gown and was measured for the support hose that she would wear as soon as she came out of surgery – a preventive measure to help circulation. She was then able to rest for a short while, wrapped in those specially heated hospital blankets. Soon they came to wheel her down the hall to the "green room" outside of surgery. Dave and I were allowed to go with her.

The large "green room," where patients are taken for final preparations, was just waking up, getting ready for the first surgeries of the day. Linda was the first patient to arrive, but by the time she was called the room was full. The staff helped her on to the surgical stretcher and started hooking up some of the monitoring equipment. They joked and talked as they went about their very serious business. One attendant was being welcomed back following a six-month medical leave for breast cancer. She would be Linda's anesthesiologist. It seemed reassuring, somehow, to have a cancer survivor taking care of Linda. She would understand.

Dr. Mollman stopped by very briefly. Dave and I said our good-byes and gave parting hugs and kisses to wish Linda luck before she was taken into surgery. We had Linda's things with us so we headed to the ninth floor and the room where Linda would be taken following surgery. Dana, a neurological nurse, and Ed, the technician who would be assisting with the mapping process, greeted us.

Ed gave us a brief tour of this sterile high-tech facility. A television camera focused on the bed where Linda would be. Monitors for this camera were in the adjacent room where Ed worked and also at the nurses' station right across the hall. Someone would be watching Linda's every move, while continually monitoring her vital signs.

Since there was nothing much for us to do, Dave and I had a quick breakfast in the cafeteria and then staked out a spot in the very crowded surgical waiting room. The same rooms were also for the intensive care ward so some families had camped out. One elderly woman had been there almost two weeks while her husband was recovering from heart surgery.

We didn't have to wait long before Dr. Mollman called Dave and me out of the waiting room and took us to a small conference room. "The surgery went well," he said, "and we have inserted the electrode band."

Linda would be sent up to her room almost immediately. We asked Dr. Mollman if he could see the tumor. "Yes," he said. "It is very large. I'd say it's probably grown 50% since the MRI in December!"

Later that afternoon, the effects of the anesthesia wore off. Linda was groggy but she could still talk. Tears started trickling down her cheeks.

"Do you hurt?" I asked.

"No. I'm just scared."

The next time she came into consciousness again, she asked, "Do I still have a brain?"

Dave was updating his mother by phone and I told him, "She's conscious again and still has a sense of humor. She wants to know if she still has a brain."

Linda touched her head gingerly and said, "No, I wasn't kidding. Do I still have a brain?"

"Of course you have a brain," I answered, holding her hand as tightly as I could.

Dave left early in the evening to pick up Jared, who had been with friends since the night before. When Linda and Dave first learned that she would need surgery, they thought they might simply explain that Mommy had gone on a trip just like Daddy did sometimes. With the help of some literature from the American Brain Tumor Association – and time – they had reconsidered and told him instead that Mommy had a bump on her head and had to go to the hospital to have it removed. He readily accepted this as he had grown up with a mommy who always wore a hat or a wig except when she was indoors with family or close friends.

I left much later. I couldn't seem to break away. I knew she was in good hands and her every move was being monitored but I just felt I had to be there. Grace, the night nurse, came on duty and came in to check her IVs. While she was doing this, we began chatting and I discovered that she was a parent from Linda's school, Mason Ridge, just a mile or so down the highway. Feeling comforted by Grace's connection with the school, I finally left to get some sleep.

January 9

WHEN LINDA CHECKED into the hospital, it was with the understanding that she would have the first surgery on Monday; they would wait a day for the swelling to go down and the mapping process would begin on Wednesday. The mapping would be done in one-hour sessions over the period of a couple of days. The second surgery would not be done until Friday. Today, therefore, was supposed to be mostly a day to let her recover from the first surgery.

Linda seemed somewhat lethargic while I was with her that morning, but that didn't seem so unusual under the circumstances. It was also about this time that I noticed – and of course people on the monitors noticed – that she seemed to be having trouble communicating. She kept trying to sit up to see the room better as if she were looking for something. Then, not seeing what she wanted, she would shrug her shoulders and lie down. I kept misunderstanding. I thought she wanted to see one of the cards that had been sent, or the flowers, or that she wanted something to eat or drink. But she would shake her head, ever so slightly because it hurt to do so, "No."

We had both just about given up when Father Corley, the priest for the ninth floor neurological unit, stopped by to introduce himself. Perhaps he could figure out what it was that Linda wanted. He started talking to Linda and then asked, "Do you have children?"

With that she nodded and said, "Bag. Bag."

"Oh, what a negligent grandma I am," I said, grabbing my purse to show Father Corley a picture of Jared. Linda smiled slightly but shrugged her shoulders as if giving up again.

"That's still not it, is it?" I said, "I wish I could figure out what it is that you want."

The phone rang. I left her bedside to answer it and give Father Corley a moment to visit with her. Again, she insisted, "Bag! Bag!"

Finally, it dawned on me – she wanted the small suitcase she had brought with her. I had put it in the closet, unopened, for it would be a long time before she would need the clothes inside. When I brought it out, she cried, "Yes! Yes!"

Inside were framed pictures of Dave and her together and of Jared. She removed these precious pictures from the suitcase, hugging them to her chest. Then we all cried with relief.

Dave had gone to work that morning because this was supposed to be simply a day of waiting. This changed suddenly when Cynthia, the head nurse, came in and asked if I could reach Dave at work. Dr. Mollman, it seemed, wanted to have a conference with us.

Dave arrived within minutes of receiving the call. We walked down the hall together to the room that served as a combined conference and waiting room. It did not look good. Too many people were gathered for this to be an informal meeting: Dr. Mollman, Dana, the nurse, Cynthia, the head nurse, Farther Corley, a social worker and a couple of other people whom I didn't recognize.

Dr. Mollman began the meeting, explaining that he was concerned because the tumor seemed to be so large and so fast growing. To add to the problem, Linda seemed to be losing the ability to speak. On consultation with Dr. Rosenfeld, they had agreed that the mapping process should begin immediately – at 3:30 p.m. that day. They would go as far as they could. Dr. Mollman was going to try to rearrange his surgical schedule so that Linda's second surgery could be first the next day, Wednesday morning. He hoped to be able to remove about 90% of the tumor. He warned that we might need to be prepared to make some quality of life decisions pending what they found. Hospice was mentioned for the first time.

Dave asked if he could bring Jared in to see his mommy while they were doing the mapping. "Yes. In fact, he might even help lift her spirits and keep her awake." The process was going to be so condensed and so intense, this was an issue.

I asked if I should call Linda's father and have him return from Sanibel. "Yes," they advised, "We think he would want to be here."

For the first time, I realized what I should have known much earlier. This was definitely not routine surgery. This was complicated, exceptional and risky!

DAVE LEFT TO pick up Jared at pre-school. I called Lamar in Florida and told him to get on a plane as fast as he could. When I got back to Linda's room, Ed, the technician, was already moving equipment into the room. Dr. Rosenfeld arrived shortly thereafter. By the time the "mapping" began, the room was full of both equipment and people. More people were stationed outside at the monitors. The band of electrodes that had been implanted the day before was now hooked up to one of Ed's machines so that Linda's responses could be measured. Her answers of "yes" or "no" were tentative and hardly audible. She was tiring quickly. Perhaps they wouldn't be able to do much at all.

Then Jared arrived. He hovered in the doorway, overwhelmed by all the people and equipment, then slowly moved to Linda's bedside. Linda's eyes reached out for a hug which was all she could physically do. All Jared could do on that first trip was to just barely touch her arm. He wanted no part of getting up on the bed. He was there only a minute or two and then was anxious to leave. Besides having to adjust to all the people and equipment, Linda didn't look like "Mommy." The surgery seemed to have drained any expression from her face. She could barely whisper and then only a word or two. And, of course, she had a huge turban-like bandage on her head. The strange-looking, multi-colored electrode band spewed out of the bandage, connecting Linda to the monitors.

On his second trip to the room, Jared did better. With some encouragement, he got up on the bed, then leaned over to get a better view of the electrode band. "Is that your rainbow?" he asked.

Jared had picked up on the beautiful way that Dave had chosen to explain the band of wires coming out of Mommy's bandage. I looked around to see tears of emotion in the eyes of the crowd of people now gathered in the room, at the doorway and at the monitors outside, to see what Jared would do.

Jared visited only about five minutes each time. Then Dave and I took shifts keeping him entertained – in the hall, in the cafeteria and in the gift shop – anything to keep this energetic four-year-old occupied while the procedure continued. Every forty-five minutes or so, we'd return. As Dr. Rosenfeld was to explain later, Jared's appearance would revive her and then they could continue for another round. This little guy was definitely doing his part to help his mommy get through this.

On the third trip, he presented her with a little angel he had chosen for her in the gift shop. Of course, he also showed her the toy car he just had to have for himself. The fourth and last trip into Linda's room was well past his bedtime. This time, he finally got up his courage. He not only got up on the bed, straddling her legs, but also reached over and gave her a hug. "I love you, Mommy."

Again, not a dry eye was to be seen in the room or the doorway.

Around 10:30 that evening, Dr. Rosenfeld called a halt to the procedure. Linda was simply too tired to continue. He hadn't gotten as much information as he would have liked, but he did have some data to guide Dr. Mollman during surgery the next day.

January 10

DAVE AND I arrived at the hospital early to wish Linda good luck before she headed to surgery. Dr. Mollman had been able to rearrange his schedule so Linda would be first – at 7:30 a.m. Later I would learn that the man who was delayed until noon that day was a neighbor of ours – just another of the many coincidences that would occur.

Lamar was flying in but wouldn't arrive until late afternoon. Good friends were going to pick him up at the airport and bring him to the hospital. Dave's family would have been here too except for the fact that his dad, Rick, was undergoing triple by-pass surgery on this very same day. Just what Dave needed was a little more stress to add to this already stressful day!

To keep occupied while we waited, I retreated to one of the small conference rooms, using the phone provided and my cell phone to call family, friends and anyone else who would listen. I called the American Brain Tumor Association and talked to a social worker to see what resources they might have. I called a clinical trial in New York that was experimenting with a new kind of laser surgery to see if Linda might be eligible for that if Dr. Mollman was unsuccessful. I was told that any tumor over three centimeters in diameter was too large to be considered. That ruled Linda out. I was riding through a storm, searching for a port, a light or some ray of hope.

I called Amy, the former friend and minister Linda and I had seen at church on Christmas Eve. I wasn't even sure she would remember Linda but it was worth a try. Amy wouldn't be back until the following week but her secretary said she would let her know. Would we like another pastor to come? "No," I replied, "I just thought Linda might enjoy talking to Amy, as she was a friend."

Too soon, I thought, Dr. Mollman came to talk with us. The surgery should have taken four hours but he appeared in less than three. "We did what we could," he said. "We weren't able to remove as much as we wanted – only about fifty per cent of the front tumor. The tumor in the back was inaccessible. If we'd done any more we would have gotten into the gray matter in the core of the brain. That could cause severe personality changes even if we could remove more of the tumor. We inserted some Gliadel wafers that will act as a chemotherapy. They may help. But I have to warn you, this is one of the fastest growing tumors I've ever seen. Without looking at the pathology slides, I would say that she may have only three to six months to live."

Dave and I were both left in a state of shock.

As I WALKED out of that conference room, I felt I had to talk to someone immediately. I grabbed my cell phone and called my friend, Jan, the first person I could think of whose number I knew. She couldn't leave school just then but would come when she could. I tried unsuccessfully to call some other people, but was too distraught to remember many phone numbers or know who to call. At almost precisely that moment, Donna appeared. Donna was my successor as president of Missouri NEA. We had been friends, but had lost touch due to her busy schedule and my changed status to retiree. Jan knew she was in town and had been able to reach her. Now, here Donna was, just when I most needed someone for moral support.

I don't know what Donna's plans were for that day but she stayed. Others started arriving. Soon we moved our group into one end of the cafeteria. Here the ICU staff could find us. Here we could cry, laugh nervous laughter and cry again, without disturbing the others in the ICU waiting room. Those people all knew our story by now. Our news was not good. I'm sure they were praying that their loved ones would do better.

Finally we were able to go up to ICU on the floor above to see Linda. She was still very groggy from sedation. I placed the pictures of Dave and Jared that I had brought from the room on her bedside table – I didn't want her to go through that frustration again. I also gave her the angel Jared had given her the day before. She reached for the small wooden figure and clutched it tightly to her chest. Tears were visible in the corner of her closed eyes. Then I left so she and Dave would have some time alone.

When I returned with a couple of the friends that had gathered, she was trying to say something but couldn't talk. The nurse handed her a signboard with the letters of the alphabet on it and common requests – turn me over, a glass of water, a face in pain. Nothing in the pictures was right. Linda made an attempt at pointing to the letters to spell something but couldn't do it. Finally, she took the marker we handed her and drew a very rough sketch. "A toothbrush? Is that what you want?"

"Yes!" Linda cried, clearly and distinctly.

LINDA'S ICU NURSE had told us that we didn't need to observe the normal rules for visitors in ICU. She understood our plight. Except for very close friends, most of our visitors stayed in the cafeteria while we returned in groups of two or three, never staying too long but just letting Linda know that we were there. On one trip to the ICU that Dave and friend Mark Bierk made, Mark reported that Linda woke up long enough to ask, "Rick?" She wanted to know how Dave's dad's surgery had gone. Here Linda was in ICU, worrying about someone else!

The next time I went to ICU, the nurse said, "She's been trying to tell me something for the past hour and I can't figure out what it is. Perhaps you can help."

With me on this visit were some of our mutual teaching friends, including Jan, who had finally been able to get away from work. We decided that perhaps a modified game of "Twenty Questions" would help and so we pursued that route. But Linda was having a hard time with "yes" and "no" and kept looking over to the left side of her bed. She pointed at the air duct on the side wall. We told her that's what it was. She shook her head but kept looking in that direction. This went on for about twenty minutes. Although she couldn't speak,

Linda made it quite obvious that she didn't want us to leave until we had solved the puzzle.

Finally, Jan commented, "Does anyone else find that radio annoying?"

"Yes! Yes!" Linda shouted, clearly and distinctly and with tears of relief.

As is so often done in ICU units, a radio or television is kept on to help the patient keep track of time. But as it happened, at this particular time, it was Rush Limbaugh's show. The radio was on ever so softly just through the headphone so as not to disturb other patients – out of Linda's line of vision but right next to her left ear. To my very liberal-minded daughter, this was one of the most raucous noises she could have heard.

With the mystery solved and the radio off, we returned to the cafeteria.

THROUGHOUT THE DAY the vigil continued. Friends came and went. Our cell phones were in constant use as we let other friends and family members know what was happening and asked for their prayers and support.

On one of my trips up-stairs to the ICU, I told Linda that her father was coming. She gripped my hand in re-lief and in gratitude. Lamar arrived late that afternoon and burst into tears as soon as he saw me. He hadn't heard the results of the sur-gery until now, for he had been en route from Florida since early morning.

We went up to the ICU together but didn't stay too long. He tried to joke and

Linda and her daddy, Lamar,
August 1, 1992.
a very special relationship

tease as he often does, but was just too distraught. Linda was the little girl he had taken care of during the afternoons of her kindergarten year while I taught. She was the little girl he would be home for after school as she went through the elementary grades. She was the little girl he had watched grow into a beautiful young woman and escorted down the aisle on her wedding day.

Linda was his little girl and her prognosis was not good.

January 11

LAMAR AND I BOTH stayed with Dave that night, although none of us slept well. I woke up in the very early hours of the morning and decided to go back to the hospital. Lamar was going to go out to our house and turn the heat and hot water on before returning. When I got to the hospital, I discovered that Dave was there ahead of me. How long he had been there, I don't really know. But he sat in silence on one side of her bed, holding her hand. I took up a post on the other side as we waited for daylight.

Before I arrived, Dave had asked the young – and expectant nurse – how ICU nurses could keep doing this, day after day, taking care of so many people whose lives hung in the balance. She told him that you do get hardened, but every now and then a patient comes that breaks down your defenses. Linda was one of those. She told Dave that she had mentioned Linda to her husband the night before and that she hadn't slept well because she couldn't get Linda out of her mind. She was the same age as Linda had been when she was expecting Jared.

Dr. Mollman came by, making his early morning rounds. He stopped to read the pathology report and the x-rays before he came to check on Linda. He pulled us aside, once again. He described the tumor as a Grade IV glioblastoma. From what I had read on the Internet and in literature from the American Brain Tumor Association, I knew this was the worst possible kind of tumor. I remembered – or hoped I remembered – that glioblastomas were still curable if caught in time.

And then Dr. Mollman told us, "The pathologist agrees – this is the fastest and most aggressive tumor we have ever seen!"

❖ ❖ ❖ ❖

ABOUT NOON, LINDA was released from ICU. We returned to the ninth floor neurological unit and a private room at the end of the hall. I retrieved the flowers that Ed, the technician, had so graciously stored in his equipment room. Laura, Linda's high school friend, maid of honor and also a teacher in another district, had been with us the day before. She returned today both during her lunch break and after school. She was cheerful and wonderful company, and in just as much pain as we were.

After school, other teachers arrived. With Linda's school so close to the hospital, teacher visits would become the norm. As to student visits, Linda had made it clear that she didn't want to have them see her in the hospital. She thought they might worry too much. So the kids worked out another way to let her know they were thinking of her. They created posters about themselves. Each poster contained their photo and then, using each letter of their name, they used adjectives to describe themselves. Some were more accurate than others, Linda later explained.

I give Lisa, Linda's substitute teacher, great credit for being so understanding. Linda had always had a strong bond with her students, but the connection with this particular group of students – and their parents – was even stronger. She and her teaching partner, Debbie, had had the same group of students for two years, moving with them from fourth grade to fifth – "looping" as it is called in the jargon. Not only had Linda had these kids for a year-and-a-half, it was also an ideally small class of only eighteen students. These kids were her extended family.

The posters arrived that afternoon. We posted them on the walls, all around the room, and even on the windows. Cards and balloons and stuffed animals and more flowers arrived. A host of angel figures arrived, too, for angels had become symbolic to Linda. Teaching partner Debbie brought two "sister" angels. "Now," she said, "You even have a Jewish angel watching over you."

Some of this display could be seen from the parking lot outside; more could be seen from the long hallway approaching Linda's room. It was quickly becoming evident to staff and other visitors alike that this room was occupied by someone very special and that person must be a very special teacher.

LINDA DIDN'T APPEAR to be in any pain but she was very pale. Her dazed, expressionless gaze made me wonder if we would ever see her smile again. Most disturbing, she had totally lost all speech. She could not even answer the question, "What is your little boy's name?" Dr. Rosenfeld tried to reassure us that speech would come back when some of the swelling on the brain went down. He also said that the tumor was centered very close to the area of the brain that controls speech. It would be awhile before we would know for sure.

Responding "yes" and "no" consistently was still not possible, and Linda found storyboards and alphabet boards confusing and frustrating. So we developed our own method of communicating. One of us would simply hold her hand, and she would squeeze to give her response. We became quite adept at doing this. That evening when Jared came to visit, we showed him how to talk with his mother, too.

We still had to address the question of what to do next. Dr. Mollman had said that Linda had three to six months to live if we didn't do anything else. Chemotherapy might give her six to nine months. It was clear that Linda was going to need some cutting edge treatment and even that might not work. I don't know that any of us – Dave, the doctors, or Lamar and I – ever fully shared the prognosis with Linda. We just didn't want her to give up hope. I'm sure she knew. She just had to look at the swollen, red eyes of everyone close to her, particularly her dad.

Gradually the visitors left, including Dave and Jared and Lamar. I simply couldn't bring myself to leave. The small reclining chair in Linda's room seemed like a viable option. I pushed it next to her bed where I could hold her hand and let her know that I was still there. When one of the night nurses came in to check on Linda, she offered to bring me a cot and I gratefully accepted. I soon found that sleeping in wool slacks in a heavy wool sweater on a plastic mattress doesn't yield a good night's sleep. Besides, I was awake every time someone came into her room, which was frequent during this first night out of ICU. But I couldn't have been anywhere else. My one and only child was sick and she needed me. And I needed her.

January 12

THIS WAS THE day that Linda had originally been scheduled for her second surgery. Were we ahead of schedule or behind? At this point it was hard to tell.

Linda woke up hungry. She'd had hardly anything to eat the last few days and was looking forward to breakfast. She had just had a bite or two when her face started twitching and she dropped the spoon she was holding in her left hand – the only hand she could use. I rang for the nurse who came in a matter of seconds. I stood on one side of the bed holding Linda's good hand, the nurse on the other, and we watched the clock. Five minutes, then ten, then fifteen. "How long does a seizure last?" I asked.

"It's hard to say," replied the nurse, "because they can vary."

And so we watched and waited. The nurse assured me that this was quite normal after brain surgery. Linda wouldn't be in any pain and might also be able to hear us talking even though she couldn't respond. Finally, fifty minutes later, the seizure stopped. Now she was too tired for the cold breakfast and went back to sleep.

My adrenaline was racing. Seizures may be normal occurrences for hospital people – but not for me. I had noticed that my ankles were swollen and thought I should probably get my blood pressure checked. That certainly wouldn't be a problem here. Plenty of nurses were around to volunteer. It was almost noon before I got around to having it checked. When I did, my blood pressure had skyrocketed. My doctor, whose office was in the same complex, warned me to take care of myself, then doubled my blood pressure medication.

That afternoon we met Dr. Cuevas, the chemo-oncologist who would be handling the next phase of Linda's treatment. He had been recommended because he was part of a very reputable oncology group at St. Luke's and he was young. Dr. Rosenfeld and Dr. Butler felt he might be more progressive in his approach than others. We liked him immediately.

He had reviewed Linda's MRIs and records. He had also consulted with Dr. Prados, chief of neuro-oncology at the University of California in San Francisco and the same doctor that had treated the son of my colleague, Karen. He was cautiously optimistic that PCV, a very powerful chemo, would help. Ordinarily, he told us, he would wait to begin the chemo until Linda had had more of a chance to recuperate from the surgery. Since Linda's tumor was so large and so aggressive he felt the treatment should begin immediately.

"What are the odds," I asked, "that this will work?"

"I really can't say," was his reply. "The odds are probably about forty to fifty per cent, but each case is individual."

We had to give it a chance. The first dose, two powerful oral capsules, was scheduled for the following Monday.

Later that same afternoon, Linda had another seizure. Although the cot hadn't been all that restful the night before, I had to stay another night. This time, I changed into one of those "beautiful" hospital gowns to be more comfortable. I woke as Linda went into the third seizure for that twenty-four hour period. As I stood by the bed holding her hand, the night nurse chuckled and commented, "Nice outfit!"

The next day I had Lamar bring me an overnight bag. I couldn't bear to leave as long as Linda was this unstable. Besides, the hospital didn't seem to mind having an extra pair of watchful eyes on duty. I might as well be comfortable. I just made sure that I was up and showered early enough – and that was very early – to be completely ready by the time the hospital's day began.

The Weekend

THE REST OF the night and Saturday morning was uneventful. Linda had no more seizures, just a few facial twitches. She had plenty of visitors that day so I decided to leave the hospital and get a haircut. When I returned, I learned that she'd had another seizure – this one lasting seventy minutes. Even if these are "normal" to hospital people, they're scary to the rest of us. I couldn't leave again.

Still, Linda had no speech and no movement or feeling in her right hand. Her right foot had started drooping, a symptom of being in bed too long. Dave had followed the nurse's recommendation, bringing in a pair of high-topped tennis shoes to help hold her foot straight. The black shoes didn't add to the glamour of her appearance but served the purpose.

Linda had brought a supply of hats to the hospital to camouflage her bandage. None of them was large enough to cover the huge turban-shaped bandage. She seemed to feel more comfortable with a hat on, even though it perched on top of her head.

On Sunday we had a steady stream of visitors. Fortunately, the hallway area outside Linda's room was wider at this point due to its location at the end of the hall. Connie, a teacher friend of Linda's and mother of Katelyn, a buddy of Jared's, had taken the kids to see "Sesame Street Live." On their return to the hospital, an attendant had obligingly wheeled a television complete with VCR to the area outside Linda's room. "Thomas the Train" videos helped keep Jared entertained.

Linda was dozing off and on as we "held court" outside her room. People who hadn't seen her were shocked by her appearance, but to my optimistic eyes, she was already looking much better. She was regaining some color and the expression in her eyes – the mirror to her soul – was returning.

One of her visitors that afternoon was George, her principal. He brought with him a copy of the letter he had sent to the Mason Ridge parents explaining Linda's condition. He also brought information about the district's insurance and death benefits, a little premature I felt, but certainly provided with the best of intentions. George had been my principal, too, prior to my leaving the district to become president of the Missouri NEA. We visited briefly and then went in to see Linda. He didn't stay long and he never came back. I know Linda thought later that was because he didn't care. I knew better. As he came out of her room, he completely broke down. As it was for so many others, it was just too difficult to see her the way she was right now.

Mid-afternoon, Dr. Rosenfeld stopped by to check on Linda. Each time he visited, he tried to get Linda to talk. He'd ask various simple and concrete questions but always began with, "What's your little boy's name?"

This time she was successful. In a hesitant tone, but clearly and distinctly, she whispered, "Jared." Happy tears followed. Being able to say "Jared" boosted her confidence so much she was able to say "glasses" and "jacket," too. Perhaps she would regain speech.

After Dr. Rosenfeld left, Linda lay back on her pillow. Her yellow hat was perched on top of her huge bandage. Black, high-topped tennis shoes graced her feet; and she was clutching a bag of chocolates a teacher friend had given to her. She could only smile with half her face so far, but smile she did, immensely pleased with herself. To some people she might have looked a little crazy. To all of us in the room, she looked absolutely beautiful.

THAT EVENING, NANCY called to say that her brother-in-law had died. He had finally lost *his* long battle with cancer. She and Jack had decided to come back from Florida to be with her sister – and Linda and all of us. "Besides," Nancy said, "we're miserable here, anyway."

So they packed their things and ours too, and drove back in our car. (They had flown to Florida because of Jack's prostrate surgery in November and he hadn't yet been cleared to drive.) There certainly was too much cancer going around in our circle, but it would be good to have them back.

January 15

LINDA HAD NOW been in the hospital for a week, but still was nowhere ready to be released. I didn't think of it until months later, but the hospital staff hadn't insisted that she get up and walk as they usually do after surgery. They knew she couldn't. They did have her sit up briefly, though. One of Dr. Mollman's assistants removed her bandage. She still had some grim looking staples in her head, but at least one of her favorite hats of choice – a ball cap – would fit now.

The chemotherapy would start today, but the big question was how to get her mobile again. Speech seemed to be returning ever so slightly, but she still had no movement in her right arm or leg. Apparently there was some doubt as to whether or not Linda would qualify for rehabilitation. She would need the recommendation of Dr. Fischer, chief of the rehabilitation department, in order to have therapy covered by her medical insurance. He was nervous about the fact that Linda was still having seizures and that she had started chemo. In order to qualify for therapy, there had to be some possibility that she could recover sufficiently for the therapy to be cost-effective. At least that's the impression I had. I can't be certain, but I think Dr. Rosenfeld was her biggest advocate in seeing this accomplished. Later we learned that Dr. Fischer was undergoing therapy for cancer himself. Perhaps this helped him ignore the odds. In any event, he placed the order for staff to do the placement screening.

During the course of the day, three different therapists – speech, occupational and physical – came to Linda's room to evaluate the appropriate starting point for therapy and to make their recommendations as to what could be done. Dave and I were both in the room when the speech therapist came. We probably should have left, but both of us wanted to make sure that this therapist knew that Linda could understand everything, even though she could hardly say anything at all. She was still my intelligent daughter and Dave's intelligent wife. It didn't matter that she couldn't answer yes or no consistently. It didn't matter that she couldn't point to her teeth and couldn't identify any letters of the alphabet. We refused to believe that these skills wouldn't return in time.

Late that afternoon, Linda was finally given Dr. Fischer's official nod of approval.

THE BIERKS ARRIVED back in town and came almost directly to the hospital to see Linda. Nancy, who had always been like a second mother – or at least a favorite aunt – to Linda, had a hard time holding back the tears. She took one look at me and made me promise that I would go to Dave's that night and sleep in a real bed.

Nancy also offered to have Jared spend the night, take him for the weekend or anything else that might help. Since Dave already had arrangements with teacher-friends that seemed to be working, I asked Linda how she felt about the Bierks helping out with Jared. As proof that Linda's verbal skills were still intact – just unavailable for the moment – Linda told us slowly but clearly, "What I want for Jared is consistency."

A few minutes earlier she'd had difficulty asking for an orange!

Consistency for Jared had been ensured for the current school year with a change in September from his day-care sitter to Love and Laughter, a pre-school and day-care center combined. Jared loved the school and seemed to thrive in their program. But there was another connection that helped during this time of crisis. Linda's friend and maid-of-honor, Laura, was also Dave's boss's daughter. Her sister, Kim, was the owner and manager of the school. Kim knew all about Jared's situation. She and her staff did everything they could to make Jared's life easier, including having him spend the night with Kim or another teacher at the school, both of whom had boys about Jared's age.

Staff and visitors alike continued to comment on the posters that covered her hospital room walls. That evening after everyone else had left, I began to read them to her, slowly going around the room. I was beginning to suspect that she couldn't read them herself but didn't have the courage to confirm my suspicions. After reading each one, I would pause and Linda would nod in agreement. Or, when a student's self perception didn't match with his or her classroom performance, she would frown slightly in disagreement. Many of the kids had also written a brief comment about how much they missed her and hoped she'd hurry back. In this way, Linda got to "read" the messages the kids had sent and I learned a lot about her students.

The concentration that this activity required wore out both of us. I waited until the 10 o'clock rounds had been made, tucked her in, and then left the hospital for the first time in three days.

By this time, the number of people who called or wanted to be called each day to be updated on Linda's condition was growing. I was running up exorbitant airtime on my cell phone, repeating and explaining the same things over and over. Thus began the *Linda Update* over the Internet. These updates would become my salvation in trying to keep so many concerned friends and relatives informed. The thoughts and prayers received in response helped keep me going. True to my reading specialist's background and training, I always tried to emphasize the positive, the good things. When I didn't have much good news to report, I simply wouldn't send an update.

Linda Update, January 17

WHAT A DIFFERENCE a few days make! While the long-term prognosis is still questionable, Linda has wonderful doctors and nurses doing everything state-of-the art possible to make her better. She has started a very powerful new chemo and will soon start rehabilitation therapy. She has temporarily lost the ability to speak and the use of her right arm. How long she will need therapy, is still unknown – it's really up to her.

Dave, Lamar, Jared and I are holding up pretty well, all things considered. Dave returned to work today. Lamar is going back out to our house where friends will help him take down our Christmas tree, not an easy task as I collect Christmas ornaments! Jared is visiting Linda every day which is good for Linda's spirit. It will also help him understand how much better Mommy is when she finally goes home.

We have now all gone through all the stages of dealing with this crisis – denial, anger, grief – and now determination! Linda licked this thing six years ago when they told her she would never have children. Now she has a four-year-old son and I have a beautiful grandson, which just shows how wrong the experts can be. As her neurologist says, they can only quote statistics. Each individual is a unique case.

We continue to take one day at a time and one step at a time but are making progress all the same. All the positive thoughts and prayers and cards mean a lot. Keep them coming!

Martha

Chapter 3

Welcome To Rehab!

THERAPY BEGAN IN LINDA'S ROOM on the ninth floor while we waited for a room to open in rehab. Since there were only eight rooms in the rehab department and patients tend to stay for a longer period than normal hospital visits, we'd have to wait our turn. As soon as her regular therapists could work her into their schedule for the full program, she would have three half-hour sessions, morning and afternoon, five days a week. On Saturdays she would have therapy only in the morning. Recreational and activity therapy was also to be part of the program.

Trish would be Linda's physical therapist, working with Linda's leg, balance and mobility. Barb was the occupational therapist. She would work with Linda's right arm but also work with her – and us – on the everyday tasks of getting dressed, going to the bathroom and taking a shower. Both of these young women were about Linda's age. We also discovered that Barb was a cousin of the Missouri D.A.R.E. officer who had worked with and nominated Linda for the D.A.R.E. award. Rapport was established immediately.

One of the first things Barb did was measure Linda for a wheelchair to make sure she had a chair that "fit" properly. She also helped Linda transfer to a chair for the first time and sit up for awhile. The wheelchair arrived the next day and we used it to tour the rehab facility on the floor below. The rehab unit looked like any other hospital floor with a few exceptions. There was a "day room," used during the day for activity therapy, and in the evening as a place for patients to go with their families to regain some sense of normalcy. A washer and dryer were provided for patients' personal laundry – a sign that these patients generally stayed in the hospital awhile. There was also a small "gym" or therapy room, used mostly for the Saturday therapy sessions. The main therapy facilities were on the ground floor of the hospital.

The patient rooms were also set up differently than most hospital rooms. Orthopedic bars stretched over the beds which were pushed close to the wall, leaving enough space in between for two patients to sit side-by-side in wheelchairs and still have room to maneuver. A small "dresser" composed of wire baskets provided storage space for patient's clothing. Bedside commodes were standard equipment in every room, as a goal of rehab was to help people be as independent as possible.

Lynn would be her speech therapist three days a week with another therapist on the alternate days. We liked Lynn's approach better than the therapist who had done the screening. Perhaps it was a matter of style or perhaps it was the nature of the speech screening process as opposed to regular therapy, but Lynn never talked down to Linda. She always talked to her as one adult to another, even though she was starting at a very basic level, getting Linda to name common, everyday things shown on picture flash cards and complete simple sentences. The "small world" syndrome would surface again as we discovered that I had Lynn's son for reading for a short period at Mason Ridge, years before.

Linda's speech difficulty resembled that of stroke victims. She had a combination of aphasia and apraxia. Many stroke and head-injury victims experience aphasia; apraxia is a little more unusual. A person with aphasia has difficulty retrieving words, much like coming to a word block in normal speaking, "the I can't think of the word for it" feeling. Aphasia victims need to relearn vocabulary and language skills.

A person with apraxia knows what they want to say, remembers the words for it, but can't process the thought to translate it into speech. Spontaneous speech, such as responding to the question, "How are you today?" is often fine.

Apraxia victims need time to respond and often confuse "yes" and "no," something we had already observed. They may also start a sentence but be unable to finish it and need to be encouraged to start over. Too much noise or external stimuli, such as loud music, too many people talking at once, or even asking too many questions at one time, can frustrate or overwhelm someone with apraxia. In their frustration they may withdraw from conversation or try to remove themselves from the situation.

January 18

BY THURSDAY, THE staff decided that Linda was ready to go downstairs to the rehab gym for therapy. Trish thought she could do more with her there with the equipment that was available. A hospital volunteer arrived to help escort her. As we entered the facility, I looked around with both optimism and apprehension. I was so hopeful that the therapy would get Linda back to normal, but it was apparent that this would take a lot of hard work on everyone's part.

Dave joined us for that first therapy session. Barb showed both of us how to help Linda transfer from a bed to the wheelchair and back and gave us time to practice. An unglamorous but helpful wide belt was put around Linda's waist, both to help with the transfer as well as to serve as a safety precaution, something to grab on to, if she fell. Barb showed each of us how to position our left foot in front of Linda's right to block it from slipping, put Linda's right arm behind our neck, then on a count of three, lift. It would take some practice – and some falls – to become proficient, but hopefully those falls would be to the bed and not the floor.

Trish had fitted Linda with a special, plastic brace to hold her right foot straight. This was put on under the black, high-topped tennis shoes that really belonged to Dave. We also met Mandy, Trish's new intern, in the gym. Today they would see if they could help Linda stand at the parallel bars. With Dave holding the wheelchair behind her and Trish and Mandy bracing each leg, Linda was finally able to stand for a few seconds before she collapsed with exhaustion.

Next we went to see Lynn for speech therapy. Two things quickly became apparent about speech therapy. Speech shouldn't be scheduled last, for the more tired Linda was, the more difficulty she had. Secondly, she didn't need an audience for speech, especially me, for it made her too self-conscious. As time went on and she gained more self-confidence, I would sit in on speech occasionally, but mostly I used this time to write notes or make phone calls.

The strain and stress of doing the transfer practice with Barb, followed by the practice standing with Trish and Mandy, proved to be enough for that day. Linda literally couldn't say a word in speech. We finally gave up. Dave returned to work and Linda and I returned to her room. On the way we were told that a room in the rehab unit had become available and she could move that afternoon. We had requested a single room, both for the privacy it provides and because we knew Linda would continue to have a lot of visitors with her school and friends so close at hand. It would be a while before she could move to one of the two single rooms in the rehab unit, but at the moment the other bed in her assigned room was unoccupied.

Meanwhile, we returned to the ninth floor so Linda could have some lunch and rest before returning to therapy again. As I wheeled her down the long hall towards her room, we both noticed that she had a visitor. A teacher friend who traveled from one Parkway school to another midday had stopped for a visit. Her timing couldn't have been worse. Linda was exhausted from the strain of her first full therapy session. She was also hungry and ready for a much-needed nap before she headed for afternoon therapy. When it became evident that the friend intended to stay for awhile, I finally interrupted.

As I walked with the visitor towards the elevator, she mentioned that she came by this way everyday about noon and could stop in. I knew that therapy was going to prove exhausting, especially at first, and Linda would really need that noon break for lunch and some rest. As tactfully as I could, I suggested that coming later in the day would be better. I guess my attempted diplomacy didn't succeed, for she never returned. If she reads this someday I hope she'll understand. I was just a mother bear protecting my cub, something I would continue to feel compelled to do at times with both visitors and hospital staff. Even though Linda couldn't speak for herself, yet, I could.

❀ ❀ ❀ ❀

WITH HELP FROM some of the wonderful nurses and hospital aides on the ninth floor, we moved to rehab that afternoon. Linda still hadn't been able to take a nap and that was the first thing she wanted to do. She had just gotten settled when Sue, one of the lead nurses of rehab, walked in.

"Welcome to rehab!" Sue said, followed by, "What? You're taking a nap? This is rehab. We don't take naps here. You should be sitting up in a chair!"

Again mother bear came to Linda's defense. "She has to have a nap," I explained. "She had an exhausting morning with the first therapy session and she's supposed to go back at 2:00." Besides, I wasn't to the point yet where I could transfer her to a chair by myself.

"All right," Sue relented, "we'll let you off the hook on your first day." She gave us a brief explanation of the rehab routine and then left.

"What a drill sergeant!" I commented to Linda as soon as Sue left, and found myself missing the compassionate staff on the ninth floor.

Linda finally got her nap and then went for afternoon therapy. I used the time she was gone to face the formidable task of moving all the things that had accumulated during her stay from the ninth floor to her new room on the eighth. Even though the other half of her new room wasn't occupied yet, we still had to save the space for the inevitable possibility.

I carefully took down all the posters from students. Debbie, Linda's teaching partner, took these back to school and had them laminated and placed in a spiral binder since we wouldn't have all the wall – or window – space we had before. But teachers are notorious for collecting stuff. They are also very generous. We still had to find places in half the space for all the balloons, stuffed animals, baskets of fruit and candy, as well as the abundance of cards and flowers she had received.

Somehow, I managed to squeeze everything into the space defined by the curtain that divided the two beds and had it ready for Linda's return from therapy just an hour or so later. Again, she needed a nap – we didn't tell Sue. After a short rest she was ready and happy to see the teachers who had stopped by after school. With the creativity teachers have to make do with what we've got, we soon discovered that the bedside commodes served perfectly well as extra seating for visitors.

Linda and I both noticed that she was the youngest person in the rehab. With the exception of one pleasant, younger man, a stroke victim in his early forties, most patients were in their sixties or older. If the other half of Linda's room were to be occupied, the patient would probably be an elderly person.

I was just getting ready to leave that evening, when someone from the hospital popped their head in the door and said that Linda was getting a roommate. I waited to see who it would be and then a very elderly woman was wheeled in. Her misshapen form made it obvious that she had suffered a severe stroke and she was moaning loudly. My heart sank and I held Linda's hand tightly as we waited to see how long the moaning would continue.

Five minutes later nurse Sue appeared in the door. She took one look at the woman in the other bed and said, "How did she get in here? She's supposed to be in the room next door." The woman was quickly moved and Sue came back to apologize. She told us that as long as another room was available, she would try to keep the other bed in Linda's room free.

Earlier we had dubbed Sue the "drill sergeant" and that nickname stuck between the two of us. But this small act of compassion – and others that would follow – made us realize that the tough act was purposeful, done to encourage the rehab patient's independence. Beneath that surface was a very caring person and a wonderful nurse.

BATHING AND THEN dressing were the next challenges Linda had to face. On the ninth floor she'd had bed baths with both a nurse and an aide assisting. On the eighth floor it was "do-it-yourself." An aide would help if you needed it, particularly getting into and out of the shower (equipped with a bench), but the aide had six to eight other patients to help, too. All rehab patients needed to be fed, showered, dressed and ready to go to therapy by 9:00 a.m.

Some days that first week or so, Linda's occupational therapy for the morning would be in her room. Barb would come to the floor and show Linda – and me – techniques to make the showering and dressing process simpler and safer. We bought tennis shoes that fastened with velcro to replace the high-tops and sweatpants outfits that could be easily slipped on and off. These all helped but still there were days when the simple act of getting dressed was exhausting. To complete the process, from bed to shower to being fully dressed, could require as many as five or six transfers.

Dave's motto for Linda was, "Bigger, faster, stronger!"

Mine was, "One day at a time, one step at a time."

We were both right.

Linda made rapid gains those first few days in therapy. Exercises that the therapists did with her would reteach the brain to read the signals coming from her arm and leg. We don't learn these things overnight initially and they aren't relearned overnight either. Very quickly she was able to step up with her left foot, assisted by the therapist. She progressed then to being able to shift her weight from her left foot to her right, something we take for granted when we walk. Intern Mandy even played

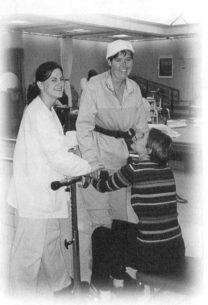

Trish and intern Mandy: celebrating Linda's first walk since surgery.

a modified bean bag version of basketball with her, with Linda standing at the parallel bars the whole time. Aside from the fact that Linda was the only youthful patient in rehab, Mandy was so impressed with her she asked to use Linda as her subject for her senior project at the university. Linda readily agreed.

Linda also seemed to be getting some purposeful movement in her right arm. As we chatted while Barb exercised Linda's arm, she would explain that Linda would first regain the movement in her shoulder, then in her arm, then her hand and finally the fingers, as her arm would wake up, section by section.

Activity therapy started with Brenda, another therapist. Linda and I (for I usually was with her) were reluctant participants at first. Linda was supposed to go to the dayroom for activity therapy right before lunch, too, and then stay and have lunch with the others. Although it was always

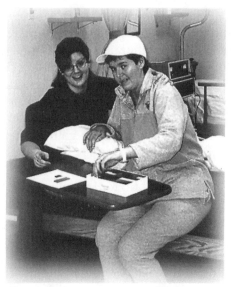

Linda working with Barb for occupational therapy.

available and Linda always felt invited, she preferred to use this time to rest. Unlike some of the patients in rehab, Linda was fortunate to have a steady stream of visitors in the afternoons and evenings. Quite frankly, we both needed the peace and quiet during lunchtime.

Brenda was flexible and managed to schedule Linda for other times, often later in the afternoon. We grew to like and appreciate Brenda as she demonstrated how sensitive she was to Linda's needs and interests. With Brenda, Linda made brownies and played games, all giving us a sense of returning to normal. Brenda also sought from me the somewhat complicated recipe for Linda's poppy seed bread and worked with the hospital to acquire the ingredients. With Brenda's help, Linda made three loaves of the bread, which were distributed to the staff in rehab and on the eighth floor. Neither Linda nor Brenda mentioned it, but I noticed that she was unable to read the measurements on the very same recipe she had made over and over again just a few weeks before.

Regaining speech and language was the hardest and most frustrating hurdle. Imagine a teacher who loves to read and to teach others the joy of reading. Imagine a mother who loves to read to her own four-year-old, sharing with him the joy of reading and nurturing his interest in language and books. Imagine this same young woman being unable to read or write or talk. In fact, she didn't even know the names of the letters. As I would comment to others frequently, "I used to think paralysis was bad . . . and it is. Far worse, however, is losing the ability to communicate."

Little by little, Linda began to regain these skills. In one of her first sessions with Lynn, she completed the sentence, "I like to drink . . ." with "Chardonnay." She still had a sense of humor.

Teacher friend Connie had given her a little basket of paper angels, each one having a "thought for the day." We made a ceremony of drawing one each day. I read them to her at first, then one day I handed it to her to see if she could read it on her own. She could and did. We both shed some happy tears.

The next day she finally felt up to reading some of the cards and notes from family, friends, parents, students and colleagues. She could read a few and I read some. One very special card arrived from a former student, Justin, who was now sixteen and in high school, complete with a photo from prom night. Although she couldn't speak much she did say she was "just overwhelmed."

Some fifth graders wrote:

Dear Mrs. Favero,

Thank you for what you taught me in Social Studies. I learned more about geography than anyone has ever taught me. You would make each assignment more exciting every time. I wish you were my Social Studies teacher this year. You made me want to learn more and more about Social Studies! When I had a trouble, there you were helping me with problems I had. I think that you were teaching us more and more and we did not even know it. You never put down anybody. Thank you for making a difference in my life. I hope that you will be able to come back this year and teach.

Your student, Bryan

Dear Mrs. Favero,

    I hope you are getting well. How are you feeling? Social studies is going very good. I'm not trying to hurt the sub's feelings, but everyone thinks that social studies is getting boring without you. The class misses you, and that's why it is getting boring.

    I got the homework finished that I owed you. Mrs. Savel is a good sub. . .

    Well I got to go. I hope I see you pretty soon.

Bye-bye for now, Elizabeth

Dear Mrs. Favero,

    Hi, it's me Justin . . . I hope you're doing all right in the hospital. I really miss you. Even though you only taught me social studies in fourth grade, you greatly influenced me. You taught me that someone can do whatever they want, even under the hardest circumstances. There's something missing at Mason Ridge Elementary School. That something is you. Please come back. Even if you don't come back this year, come back the next. You have made a great difference here. A good difference. I will never forget you. That's a promise. And I *will* keep that promise.

Love, Justin

Dear Mrs. Favero,

    How are you doing? I am fine. I am doing well in school. It is not as fun as it would be if you were here. Mrs. Savel is nice. I miss you so much. Do you like your gift? Does Jared like the books? Mrs. Lebon and Mrs. Ford ate lunch with all the girls and the quiet girls (you know who) really spoke up. Everyone misses you. We are always thinking about you, but we are doing our best so we can make you proud. I'm going the extra mile for you. As you probably know, I got all checks on my progress reports. You wouldn't believe some of the stories we recollect from the days you were here. Even the beginning of school! I am writing a long story at home. Possibly my favorite. When I'm finished I will send you a copy. I have read many books. Are you still going to move? Do you have those headaches that you used to have?

I miss you extreme!

Love, Tracy

CONVERSATIONAL AND SPONTANEOUS speech were returning rapidly. Linda was able to tell one of the parents who visited, "I feel more comfortable than I have in weeks!" but sometimes couldn't respond to a direct question if put on the spot. This was particularly true with questions requiring a "yes" or "no" answer. We learned to wait, for she would often correct herself when given enough time. When we were together or when there was just one other person in the room, she would do well. We also discovered that she could carry on a limited conversation on the phone. We teased Linda sometimes that we might have to call her up when she got stuck trying to tell us something. Too many people in the room or too much extraneous noise, and she would withdraw. These situations were just too confusing to her. She was also inconsistent. She could express a complex thought one minute but might have difficulty telling us she had a headache the next. All of these tendencies were characteristic of apraxia, Lynn continued to reassure us.

Linda was in rehab for less than a week when Dr. Butler stopped by for a visit. He had overheard a conversation Dr. Fischer was having about this new, young patient in rehab who was doing so well. This was before Dr. Fischer realized that Dr. Butler was Linda's doctor, too. We felt she was doing well, too. We hoped that this would be confirmed by the MRI that Linda would have at the end of January. In the meantime, she worked her heart out in therapy and continued with powerful doses of chemo.

ON THAT FIRST Sunday in rehab, Linda had a roomful of visitors. She still didn't have a roommate so there was plenty of room. Jared had come down with a mild case of hives – his reaction to stress I guess – and was so tired he fell asleep on the floor, oblivious to the conversations around him. With Linda surrounded by friends and family, I left to go home for the first time. It was time to face unpacking from Florida, then repack to stay in town, although now I would be staying with the Bierks. It just seemed to be less stressful than staying with Dave and Jared.

Jared responded by coming down with a tummy virus so "Grandma Nancy" came to the rescue. The next night I did stay with him and we had a wonderful "picnic" in the dining room – by his request. This was something "my mommy does with me."

Mason Ridge parents continued to come by. So as not to overwhelm Linda too much, a few had been selected as the designated visitors. About this time, teachers and parents together set up a catering service for us, delivering evening meals to the hospital several nights a week. We were able to take these meals to the dayroom and take advantage of a nearby microwave for re-heating. We soon found we had to suggest that people not send quite so much!

Teachers stopped by for a visit in groups and individually on their way home from school. The Mason Ridge teachers reported that the Student Council had decided to make the American Cancer Society the beneficiary of their fund-raiser that year. They also said that the school recycling effort, which Linda had started, had been given an added boost with her hospitalization. Everyone wanted to do something. The teachers, themselves, had made a get-well video for Linda, a tour of the school with every staff member wishing her well. Teachers from Pierremont, the school where she had taught previous to Mason Ridge, visited too, and brought an autographed bear to wish Linda well.

Linda had us tell the school that she wasn't up to seeing student visitors but one afternoon we received a phone call. It was Ruth, mother of Justin-the-prom-goer. Not only had Linda had Justin as a student, she had also had his younger brother, Josh, and would have had his youngest brother, Jared – and yes, that is Jared's namesake – the following year. The boys had been asking about Mrs. Favero and Ruth asked if it would be all right if they came by for a few minutes. Linda relented.

Linda now had a roommate, a sweet elderly woman. Linda didn't want to disturb her so we met Justin and his family near the elevators. Justin presented her with a charming, little bouquet of roses nesting in a birds-nest basket. Although these were real roses, they never died, just faded a little as they dried, symbolic I think. That little bouquet is still in the breakfront of Dave and Linda's home.

Even though it was only for a few minutes, I think the visit convinced Linda that kids could be pretty tough and that seeing her was reassuring to them and helped her, too. She still wasn't ready to send an open invitation. Her students continued to send messages and pictures. Since we had little wall space in our half of the room, the kids mounted photos of them – and her – on a large poster-board that we could display and move around as needed. The acrostic posters that had been both amusing and comforting on the ninth floor were now laminated and in a spiral binding. Each day we would hang a new one over the orthopedic bar over her bed. The student whose poster rose to the top that day was our "student of the day" and an incentive to keep working.

One child found another very special way to communicate. Mara wasn't even a student of Linda's. She was the second grade sister of fifth grader, Ben, who was in Linda's class. Mara's teacher, Mary, stopped by after school one day. She waited and waited while other teachers visited with Linda. After they left, she stayed. In fact, Linda was getting very tired and I suggested that she might need to rest before dinner. There had been a lot of visitors that day. Mary left the room and then came back and signaled me from the door. She'd been waiting to see me alone – without Linda. She had a poem that Mara had written and wasn't sure that Linda would be up to seeing it. I told her that I thought Linda would appreciate it and, without looking, took it into share with Linda. I didn't realize what a treasure I held in my hand until I started reading.

The Classroom is Bare

The classroom is bare because
the teacher is not there.
When the teacher is not there the
classroom is bare.
The children sit at their desks alone, working

and working as hard as they should.
So, they work and work until the teacher
Comes back.
Day after day they work very hard.
One day the teacher comes back to
Teaching with joy and happiness.
She is a great teacher.
The classroom is not bare anymore and
we are happy because Mrs. Favero is back.
I miss her very much.

Mara Lesser

❖ ❖ ❖ ❖

WHILE TEACHERS AND students were easing Linda's stress in the hospital, Dave continued to be plagued with the issue of the new home that was under construction. He'd wanted to follow Dr. Butler's advice immediately and try to get out of the contract. I'd urged him to hold off until we knew more about Linda's long-term prognosis. She was looking forward so much to that house and had so many dreams for it. Neither of us had mentioned this dilemma to Linda.

During Linda's first week in rehab, Dr. Fischer stopped Dave and me in the hall to talk to us about what we might expect. Linda would be eligible for weekend "day passes" soon, returning to the hospital each night. This was part of the rehab plan of trying to move patients towards independence.

"What is the layout of your home?"

"Two story with a half-bath and no bedrooms downstairs; two steps up to get into the house."

"Hmm. . . . you might want to consider setting up a bedroom downstairs."

Then Dave told him about the new house – which was also a two-story. Dr. Fischer reinforced what Dr. Butler had recommended, "See if you can get out of that contract. Even if Linda continues to get better, stairs may always be a problem."

We reluctantly told Linda and Dave called the builder. "No dice," said the builder. "It's yours. It will be finished mid-April and then you can sell it."

Although he certainly understood the builders' perspective, Dave was shaken by the builders' lack of compassion and furious with me for delaying things. They were going to be stuck with a house that wasn't suitable for them and that would also leave them financially strapped if they couldn't sell it. Besides, they would probably end up having to pay a realtor's fee to sell the place, something the builder would not have to do, causing them to lose still more money.

A day or two after this news, I was at the beauty shop that I've gone to since Linda was a baby. In "Steel Magnolias" fashion, the people there knew about Linda and asked how she was doing. "She's doing much better," I said and then explained the situation about the house.

In another one of those almost eerie coincidences, a man who was getting a haircut happened to be one of the big brass in the same construction company. "I'm in another division," he said, "but my brother is in charge of new home construction.

Let me see what I can do. If your son-in-law doesn't hear from us in the next few days, call me."

A few days later the builder called and offered a deal: they could trade to another house, a one floor plan, in the same subdivision. There was a display model in St. Charles they could go through to see if they liked the house. The only remaining lot in the subdivision, however, was very undesirable, having a steep embankment ending in a drainage pond. One of the reasons they had wanted to move was for Jared to have a better place to play than the steeply sloped lot they currently had.

That weekend Dave's parents, Rick and Rachel, came for the first time since Linda's surgery. Rick was still recovering from triple by-pass surgery and hadn't been able to make the drive any sooner. I knew it would be a relief to Dave to have them there and their visit would also give me a brief respite. Lamar and I have always enjoyed their company. We used to tease Dave and Linda that they had tried to pick parents that matched. Rick worked in a manufacturing company and was a union man and shift worker, just as Lamar had been. Rachel was a teacher. We all had marriages that had survived the trials of time.

With the house problem looming over them, Dave and his parents decided to drive out to the display that Friday afternoon. After they returned, Nancy and I would go for a separate inspection. We confirmed what the others had thought. The house wasn't worth wasting Linda's energy. Yes, it was a one-floor plan, but with narrow hallways that would be difficult to make handicap-accessible.

Dave called the builder again and said the house was not acceptable. They wanted out of their contract. The person he spoke to was noncommittal but did offer to see what he could do.

Linda had therapy on Saturday morning, then left the hospital with Dave on her first "day pass." As soon as she was gone, I called a local realtor from the hospital. My mission was to do some preliminary scouting that afternoon just to see if there were affordable ranch houses in the Parkway area – and preferably close to Dave's work and Jared's preschool. I explained my mission to the realtor – I wasn't the client and I didn't even know if they would be interested. Again, I was in luck. Kathy, the realtor who happened to have desk duty that afternoon, was a cancer survivor herself and sympathetic to my cause. I gave my report to Dave and Linda – yes, there were possibilities, although ranch houses sold very quickly. Soon Dave and Linda would be Kathy's clients.

THE SECOND PART of that weekend was not so successful as Linda, Dave and all of us adjusted to the challenges of handicapped living in a not-so-handicapped equipped home. Lamar and I had not gone there on Saturday in order to give Dave and Linda some quality time with Dave's family. On Sunday, we were later than we expected because of icy roads in our rural setting. We arrived at lunchtime, to sounds of Dave shouting, "Jared, be quiet." Dave brought Linda a sandwich in the living room where she was sitting on the couch. Dave had helped her transfer from the wheelchair to the couch for a change of pace, but that meant that she was unable to get up and move on her own. I sat down with her and waited, thinking the others would join us, bringing their lunch into the living room, too. They were in the kitchen – out of sight but not out of hearing range – carrying on normal everyday conversations. But Linda was not part of them. This wasn't intentional, just an adjustment we would all have to make.

"Would you like to join them?" I asked.

Linda nodded affirmatively, tears in her eyes. That meant I had to call Dave in to help get Linda from the couch to the wheelchair. She didn't have enough strength in her legs for me to make that transfer yet. Dave did so willingly, but in a manner that spelled, "tension."

To add to the stress, Linda's wheelchair did not fit into the half-bath in the hall. Dave had to take her to the door, help her get up and then help her shuffle to the toilet. The process had to be repeated in reverse afterwards. On one such trip Linda had an accident. "Why didn't you tell me sooner?" said Dave to Linda who had difficulty talking anyway and more when there was stress. On another trip to the bathroom Dave discovered that the chair's wheels were making marks in the new kitchen floor that had been installed just before Christmas. It was too much. In frustration, he shouted angrily about the marks on the new floor, then went upstairs where he and Jared spent most of the afternoon watching the Super Bowl.

Elaine, one of Linda's teaching team members, brought dinner that afternoon. Dave and Jared joined us for that. Dave had calmed down and dinner went peacefully and amicably, but Linda was naturally relieved to return to the peace and quiet and security of the hospital that evening.

January 29

MUCH OF THE tension that weekend had nothing to do with the house or adjusting to handicapped living. Linda's first MRI since surgery was scheduled for Monday, the twenty-ninth. It was our first chance to see what the surgery and chemo had accomplished. We had been warned that it might not show anything yet, but were hopefully optimistic just the same. We had to be.

When I arrived at the hospital early that morning, Linda was tired. I immediately jumped to the conclusion that it was the stress of the weekend and the MRI scheduled for that day. In reality, kind Mrs. Esther's radio going all night was more of the culprit. Heather, an aide who reminded me much of Linda's cousin, Sharon, facilitated the arrangements for Mrs. Esther to move to another room. "You need your rest," she said privately to us.

Linda only had time for a quick sponge bath before it was time for the MRI, a special kind this time called a Radionics MRI. We wouldn't get the results until the next day. It was just another one of those many long waits we had to endure, but so much depended on these results.

From the MRI, Linda went directly to the rehab gym. She had the full entourage today for Rick, Rachel and I were all with her. We warned Trish and Mandy that Linda was tired from the day before and nervous from the MRI. Then she surprised us all. Aided by a special half-walker and Trish, she walked for the first time. That afternoon she repeated the performance. The next day she was able to expand her walk to forty feet at a time – still assisted but with her doing more of the work herself. It was with this optimism that we waited for the results of the MRI. Something had to be working right!

January 30

LINDA HAD A good night's rest and was in an optimistic mood. We drew three "angels of the day" to catch up and headed for therapy. She had a good speech session and then walked another forty feet.

Rick and Rachel came to watch morning therapy. They planned to stay for the appointment with Dr. Butler and then return to Lockport. At 12:30 we headed to radiation oncology and waited to see Dr. Butler. Lamar and Dave joined us there. We now had a full entourage waiting in that small, windowless room. Lamar tried to make a joke or two to ease the tension but with no success. Linda, herself, was trying to hold back the tears. The rest of us continued to stare at the starkly bare walls or the blank institutional-gray carpeting.

We waited.

The results of the MRI could have been better. They also could have been worse. The truth was the results were ambiguous. Linda's last x-ray had been a CT scan (Computed Tomography Image) on January 9. Comparing the results of a CT scan and an MRI is a little like comparing apples and oranges. The tumors *may* be stable but the radiologist could not be certain. All three tumors, the original tumor and the two new ones, were still too large for the hoped-for stereotactic radio surgery which could have removed them completely. They needed to be much smaller and more concentrated. In fact, to do radio surgery at this point might do more harm than good. He also confirmed that all three of the tumors were now classified as glioblastoma-multiformes. I knew that Linda had done enough reading over the past few years to know that these were terms you didn't want to hear.

The doctors were noncommittal as to whether Linda's remarkable progress so far, both physically and in speech, was normal recovery from the surgery or due to less pressure from the tumors. Dr. Butler advised that the best course of action was to continue with the PCV chemotherapy – at least for two more rounds. They would do another MRI in about five or six weeks. Linda would continue with the rehab therapy as long as she continued to make improvement. Her progress would be evaluated on a weekly basis.

This was not the positive news we had hoped for, but not as bad as it could have been. Once again, we would just have to wait and see. Rick and Rachel said their good-byes and headed home. Dave left for work and Lamar left for home. Linda and I returned to her room where she opted to take the afternoon off from therapy to cry a little and regroup. With a little rest she was back to being herself, saying, "I'd like to play Parcheesi."

We started the game and Linda laughed at herself, "I didn't realize I'd forgotten how to count!" Brenda had suggested the game in activity therapy and had brought it to the room for just that purpose – to help with counting.

As I said in the *Linda Update* that evening, "It looks like we're in this for the long haul, so keep those prayers going." We certainly needed them now.

LINDA CONTINUED TO do well in therapy that week. She walked eighty feet in one stretch and was demonstrating more movement in her right arm. Speech also went well. On Wednesday she finally got her private room down the hall, after an almost two week wait. She now had a little more room for all her things, a larger, wheelchair accessible bathroom and shower, and even an accessible sink and vanity area where she could begin taking charge of her personal grooming again. With a private room also came the advantage of more space for visitors and the chance to get a better night's sleep without the complications that a roommate can bring.

While it took a few trips to bring all the things she had accumulated to her new room, aides helped and we accomplished the move quite easily. It didn't take long to reinstall the posters, the cards, the mini TV with VCR and the "Student of the Day" book to make it feel like a teacher's room again. I also brought a fresh bouquet of Stargazer lilies to brighten up the room. Linda's bridesmaids' bouquets and centerpieces for her wedding used these lilies and they still evoked wonderful memories.

Early Thursday morning the rehab team met and reported. They were recommending that therapy continue for two more weeks, pending approval from the insurance company.

That same day Linda suffered a setback. She didn't even want to take a shower. She had a headache and said she felt bad all over. She did fine in speech but physical therapy proved to be just too much. After ten minutes, Trish stopped the session and we went back upstairs.

"Was this a tumor headache?" I wondered.

I had just gotten Linda in bed when Brenda came by and offered to do a relaxation exercise with us. She played some beautiful nature music. The music, the soothing talk of the relaxation exercise, and the fragrance of the Stargazer lilies were just what Linda needed to relax. She slept for over an hour, had lunch and then returned to therapy with renewed energy and determination.

Dave called that afternoon to ask if Lamar would be in that evening. He'd had an offer from the builder and wanted to discuss it with Linda – and us. We gathered in Linda's room and Dave explained the offer. The builder would try to sell the house, beginning immediately. When they did, Dave and Linda would get their money back. All of it! Dave was so concerned about Linda's reaction that he was talking non-stop, as if he needed to convince her. Lamar kept adding reasons to take the offer, too. Neither of them were really noticing Linda's reaction.

I motioned for them to stop. "Linda, what do you think?"

Very calmly and reasonably she said, "I think we should sell the house."

We retreated down the hall to the day room to enjoy a dinner provided by two of the Mason Ridge teachers. Dave wasn't hungry and left soon after dinner. The stress of the house decision was getting to him. Lamar left, too, and Linda and I watched television. Things seemed to be peaceful enough but as I tucked Linda in for the night, she was crying. She was worried about the house and scared about the pain she was having. Without being able to say so, I knew she was mirroring my thoughts, "Can the tumor be growing this fast?"

WHEN I ARRIVED the next morning, Linda still had a headache but wanted to try going to therapy anyway. She met with Barb first for occupational therapy then went to speech. In speech, the pain was becoming too much, making it difficult for her to successfully concentrate on anything. One of the nurse's aides from the eighth floor was called to bring her some pain medication. Linda pointed to her cheek. It was puffy and swollen.

Prior to the surgery Linda had been able to distinguish between the piercing, concentrated pain of a tumor headache and the general pain most of us have with a headache. "Is this a tumor headache?" I asked.

Linda shook her head, "No."

"Can it be sinus?"

"Yes," she cried. She hadn't been able to remember the word for it.

With the relief of resolving the nature of the pain, she went on to continue her therapy. For the first time that morning she "walked" around the entire loop of the rehab department, about one hundred feet. She repeated her success that afternoon. When the Mason Ridge teachers arrived after school to visit, she was bubbling with happiness and eager to share the news of her feat, even giving demonstrations in the hallway.

Dr. Rosenfeld stopped by for a visit. It was his responsibility to monitor Linda's dilantin levels which would help prevent seizures. He assured us that he didn't think the headaches and the tumor were related.

AT NOON DAVE called to discuss arrangements for the weekend. I told him that I thought he might want some time alone with Linda. He interpreted this to mean that I didn't want to be there.

When he and Jared arrived that evening, Dave was tense. In the dayroom he didn't eat, but spoon-fed Jared who was perfectly capable of feeding himself. His tension was affecting all of us as we ate almost in silence. It was a sharp contrast to the successful and happy day Linda had been having earlier. Then Dave mentioned that Linda's friend Connie was going to come to the house Saturday evening. I replied that that might help me. I could go home for the evening.

Suddenly the stress of the past few weeks caught up with him. Dave bolted out of his seat and started yelling almost incoherently in frustration – in clear view, if not hearing range, of the nurses' station on the other side of the dayroom window. I suspect they had witnessed such scenes before as families tried to cope with long-term hospital stays and questionable outcomes. He wheeled Linda down the hall with Jared following. His anger continued in Linda's room. Linda was crying and trying to escape by wheeling herself out of the room – a typical reaction for a person with apraxia.

Neither Lamar nor I were sure what we should do. We hated to leave them – and Jared – in this state but also felt they needed to work it out on their own. I grabbed my coat and my purse from Linda's room and told them that we would be at the Bierks if they wanted us.

About 9:30 that evening I received a phone call. It was Linda. She was unable to dial the phone herself but had had one of the nurses' aides dial it for her.

As she struggled for composure she whispered, "I don't know what to do."

"I don't either," I replied. We talked briefly and then I said, "Call Dave and tell him you love him!"

It was the only thing I could think of at that moment.

On Saturday morning I arrived at the hospital early to help Linda bathe and get ready for therapy. I asked Linda if she had called Dave and she said she had. I explained to her how badly I felt and then I shared with her a letter I had written to Dave to try to explain my perspective. I just didn't think Dave would be receptive to listening after the evening before – and I was right.

Linda had speech first with the Saturday therapist. Since Linda did better without an audience for speech, I wandered down the hall to a waiting area near the elevators. I was there when Dave got off the elevator. He sat down next to me but was as tense as he had been the night before. I handed him the letter and walked to another waiting area to give him a chance to read it in privacy.

Saturday, February 3

Dear Dave:

I'm putting this in writing because I don't know what else to do.

I am very sorry about last night, especially if I did or said something that caused it. Linda had had such a wonderful day and was so pleased with herself and her progress. Unfortunately, she really didn't have a chance to share that with you, at least while I was there.

All Lamar and I, Nancy and Jack, or anyone else that has offered to help wants to do is to help you, Linda, and Jared achieve that "balance" you referred to. We want you to have the time to visit with Linda when it is quality time for both of you – when she is rested, when you can relax without constantly having to worry about Jared. We also want to help in anyway we can to help you have quality time as a family when you are together and with Jared when you and he are at home.

Apparently we are not achieving that as far as you are concerned. I thought you might enjoy – and need – having time with Linda at home today without other people present. That's why I didn't plan to stay for the afternoon. Quite frankly, I wasn't sure where or what I was going to do, I just wanted to get out of your way so you could have some space as a family – if you wanted to. When I suggested that you didn't need to leave work early to pick up Jared, it was because I know how important your work is to you and that you normally work until 5:00 p.m. or so, not to keep you away.

When Lamar "escapes" to the lake, it's because he doesn't know what he can do to help. He cares greatly about Linda – and Jared – and you. However, when he's at your house or visiting the hospital, he feels like he's just sitting around waiting – and not needed.

Please take the few minutes necessary to read the last couple of small chapters in the booklet, *Living with a Brain Tumor*. Please take the time to read the booklet, *Apraxia*. (Incidentally, this booklet is for Linda, too, although she will need to have someone read it and discuss it with her.) I don't suggest them because I'm trying to tell you what to do. I think the booklet might help you better understand the communication struggle Linda is currently undergoing. I know it helped me. The one about living with a brain tumor may offer some suggestions about how other people have coped – and things that can help.

Linda is the only daughter we will ever have. Jared is the only grandchild we will ever have. You are the only son-in-law we will ever have. All of you are very precious to us. In this very stressful time for all of us, we need to be working together, helping each other. We just need to know how we can help, what you want us to do – or not to do.

Martha

AFTER DAVE READ THE letter, he came to where I was waiting and said, "I'm going over to the Bierk's and see if I can get this straightened out." He knew that Lamar would be there, too.

Dave had felt that we were all trying to tell him what to do and when he could and couldn't visit. We had also been pushing, too much perhaps, for him to take advantage of the many offers of help that were pouring in. He didn't know the Mason Ridge parents or the teachers that were offering to help and was reluctant to accept help from strangers. Besides, as he said, the house was lonely and Jared was his company. That was certainly understandable.

Dave met with the Bierks and Lamar and then returned to the hospital to meet with Linda and me. He had calmed down and apologized, especially to me. He, Lamar and the Bierks had worked out a tentative visiting schedule, which they thought would give me a reprieve, and put less pressure on Dave as well. Some evenings Nancy would come to be with Linda so that I could go home. Some evenings Dave would come. Dave would also come for therapy and lunch once or twice a week. We'd work out weekends as they came.

I remember Linda saying to both of us, "All I want is for everyone to get along."

WITH THE ISSUES temporarily resolved and a plan worked out, Lamar and I left, and Dave took Linda home on a "day pass."

Since I was still helping Linda bathe and dress in the morning, I returned to the hospital on Sunday morning. She assured me that everything had gone well. Connie and her little girl, Katelyn, had come over as planned. Katelyn and Jared had fun together and Linda had a good visit.

We mistakenly thought that Linda was going to have an IV as part of her chemotherapy on that Sunday morning but this wouldn't be until the next day. Linda opted not to have another day pass. Jan, friend to both Linda and me, came and spent the morning with us, watching videos and joining us as Linda practiced walking in the hall. Dave came for the afternoon so Lamar and I left to give them some time together.

We knew the next day, Monday, was going to be a big day.

Chapter Four

Teacher of the Year

February 5

WHEN I ARRIVED THE NEXT morning, I was full of anticipation for we had a surprise planned for that afternoon. Debbie had called a few days earlier to say that Linda had been named the Mason Ridge Teacher of the Year. Some teachers wanted to come to the hospital after school to make the announcement. They also wanted to video her reaction and would share that with the rest of the staff the next day.

Debbie assured me that Linda's being named Teacher of the Year was not a sympathy vote. For her positive involvement with students and parents, for the recycling project that was now district wide, and for her work with Forest Park Forever, she had rightfully earned the award.

I told Dave and Lamar but had sworn them to secrecy. I also told the rehab nurses so that we could reserve the dayroom and temporarily hide some flowers. But that morning as I entered the room, Linda seemed dejected and sad. "What's wrong?" I asked.

"I am perturbed!"

I laughed at her choice of words and commented that her vocabulary was definitely coming back. "What are you perturbed about?"

As was so often the case, Linda could not immediately answer the direct question. It took a series of questions for me to discover what was wrong. Finally, she was able to tell me that a night nurse had made fun of her because of the way she talked.

"I am very upset," she said. "I am angry."

I was upset, too, but Linda was proud to be able to say that she had already reported her concern to the head day nurse. Apparently her nurse from the previous night was a part-time nurse, one who did not normally work the rehab unit. This was the first time since Linda had been in the hospital when her care had been anything other than top-notch. She was assured that she would not have that particular nurse again.

We put the matter behind us and went to therapy.

During afternoon therapy, I tried to clean up the room and dispose of faded flowers so there would be room for more. Brenda, the activities therapist, coaxed Linda into putting on a little make-up, saying some friends had arranged for the Chippendales to come to the day room.

The Mason Ridge crew was ready and waiting when we got there.

"Surprise!" they shouted, and handed her a bouquet of flowers. Debbie read the prepared announcement and

Dave and Mason Ridge teachers surprise Linda with Teacher of the Year announcement.

presented her with a poster collage from her students. Linda was both pleased and overwhelmed, saying quite literally, "I'm speechless."

Dave was on hand with a dozen red roses – which he said, jokingly, had to last until Valentine's Day. A card from Jared and him proclaimed, "You're our teacher of the year every year!"

Lots of happy-teared rehab staff were watching outside the day room window. Brenda asked for a copy of one of the photos for the St. Luke's West staff newsletter. I was one proud mom and was more than willing to oblige.

THE NEXT COUPLE of days Linda seemed very restless. She just couldn't seem to get comfortable – in her bed, in her wheelchair or even in the lounge chair in her room. This was compounded by the fact that she couldn't explain to us why or where she hurt, but she definitely wasn't OK. Nancy spent one evening with us. Both she and I would jump at Linda's every move – and move her again, trying to help. I scheduled a massage for her, thinking she'd just been in a prone position too long. That had to be cancelled after the first five minutes because she was in too much pain.

On Wednesday morning, after almost two days of questioning from me, from Dave, the nurses, and the therapists, Linda announced, "The gas has passed!"

How simple and yet how complicated when you can't tell someone where you hurt!

With that problem resolved, Linda had two great days of therapy in a row. First, she progressed from a half-walker to a "claw" cane. After one hesitant loop, she went again for 150 feet and then doubled that distance in the afternoon. The next day Trish switched her cane to a smaller base yet. She was able to accomplish the 150 feet with that, too. Trish had her practice stepping up the equivalent of one step, then nodded towards the practice stairs that were in one corner of the gym. "Are you ready to try those?"

Linda nodded in affirmation. Slowly, hesitantly and with Trish's support and encouragement, she went up the set of four stairs, turned and came back down – twice!

"I climbed Mt. Everest!" she cried – more happy tears from all of us.

We had an ice cream cone after therapy to celebrate and Linda called Dave and her daddy to share the good news.

I didn't go with her to speech but she told me, "I was awesome in speech, today!" Lynn concurred.

We showed off our shower and dressing skills to Barb. Linda put on a pair of scrub pants, unassisted, and almost tied her shoes one-handed. Barb was impressed.

Lamar came the next afternoon for therapy. Brenda took both of them outside for some fresh air and to play a game. Linda was definitely making progress.

On Thursday the rehab team met again. Linda was approved for another two weeks of rehab. That meant staying in the hospital for another two weeks, but it also meant receiving much more intense therapy than she could have at home. As she continued to progress, the day passes on weekends would be easier.

LINDA AND I were having lunch in her room when Debbie called. The kids had written a lot of congratulatory letters to her for being "Teacher of the Year" but they really wanted to see her. As one mother put it, Linda had always been so open with her students about her illness, seeing her would be reassuring. Linda wasn't sure, but buoyed by the success she had this week in rehab, agreed. We decided that a group visit for those who could come might be easier and agreed to the following Monday after school.

Linda hung up the phone (yes, she could talk some on the phone now) and we continued eating. We'd gotten adept at ordering from the special, extended menu offered to rehab patients and often shared a lunch. Perhaps it was because of all the triumphs that week or perhaps it was just because she could talk so much better now, but for the first time since her surgery she started asking questions she'd waited a long time to ask – questions about her surgery and her prognosis.

I told her as much as I could and drew the picture of the brain and explained the mapping.

"What would have happened if we'd done the surgery on December 15?"

"We'll never know."

"I don't feel like I have cancer."

I explained that there were three possibilities. "Your progress could be because you're recovering from surgery; it could be because the tumors are not growing anymore; it could be because the chemo is working. We hope it's all three."

Connie came after school, bringing her daughter and Jared's pal, Katelyn. Dave came later with Jared. The two children had great fun riding on Linda's lap in the wheel-chair. Linda proudly showed off her walking abilities to any-one who would watch: first to the teachers that came after school, then to Connie, then to Dave and Jared, and finally to Nancy who came that evening. She would repeat her perfor-mance for any new visitors that showed up during that week.

Jared and Katelin visit Mommy

Dave was much more re-laxed. The builder had of-fered to return $17,000 of their investment now, the balance when they sold the house as a "spec" house.

That evening after all the other visitors had left and Dave had gone to put Jared to bed, I shared with Linda some of the congratulatory letters the kids had sent.

Dear Mrs. Favero,

How are you? I really miss you and hope I see you soon. You won teacher of the year! I just knew you would win. We all were shouting hooray and clapping when they said you won. You are a remarkable person and teacher . . .

I can't wait to see you again! I love you and miss you!

Most love, Carolyn
P.S. I hope you are having an OK time at the hospital. Feel Better!

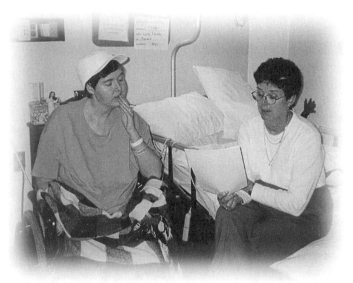

Martha reading one of the many letters from students to Linda.

Dear Mrs. Favero,

Congratulations, Mrs. Favero, you are the "Teacher of the Year." I had no clue it was going on. All the class went wild when you won. I was not surprised that you won. You're an awesome teacher. Mrs. Savel is nice but we can get out of hand.

In *Roots* we are at the sixth part. *Roots* is not what I thought it would be. It's so gross. Junte Kinte (Toby) died. It is sad and cruel and there are a lot of curse words.

In math we are adding fractions with unlike denominators. It is confusing. Get well.

Cory

Dear Mrs. Favero,

Did you know you are "Teacher of the Year?" Isn't that exciting. We learned how to add fractions. Now that is fun. I wish you were here to teach us how to add fractions. *Roots* is going fine. I find it very interesting.

I really like *Roots*. It shows a lot about slavery that I didn't know. I'm glad that we are watching *Roots* because it helps me understand slavery more than I knew.

I like Mrs. Savel. She is really nice. She seems to be doing everything fine. I wish you were here to teach us. I hope you get well soon.

Sincerely, Tyler

Dear Mrs. Favero,

Congratulations! You got teacher of the year! I definitely think you are worthy. How are you? You have to let me know as soon as you can see visitors and when I could come.

Roots is great. We've already watched parts 1,2,3 and 4. There are violent parts but we work around them.

I was sick last week. I was out Wed. Thurs. and Fri. Yipee!

We all miss you a lot. But I'm getting used to Mrs. Savel. She is a good teacher. I still think of her as a sub and hope that you will come back! Speaking of subs, we had something today that we never had before – a sub for the sub! She is nice. On the bottom of this page, I will have some artwork.

We all miss you,

Jordyn

Dear Mrs. Favero,

I've missed you so much that something that was said on the intercom about that you were Teacher of the Year and that made my day because that's the first time I heard that you were the Teacher of the Year.

The movie *Roots* is interesting . . . because it shows me how slavery was and how harsh it was to owners and slaves.

Sincerely, Tre'Nesha

Dear Mrs. Favero,

How are you? Did you know that you are teacher of the year? Congratulations! I had a feeling that you would get the teacher of the year award. We are learning a lot and Mrs. Savel is very nice, but I still wish that you were here. Things just aren't the same without you. . . . .

We all miss you very much and we are praying that you are able to come back this year.

Sincerely, Your student, Alyssa

Dear Mrs. Favero,

We miss you here at Mason Ridge. I think you deserve to get teacher of the year, of course you would be my first pick. I think you are the best teacher and hope you come back soon to teach next year. And show them how you are the best teacher because you are down right cool.

Paul

CARDS AND LETTERS began to arrive from former students and parents of students, both current and former. We read them all and then posted them on the tag board I'd brought in to help display the wonderful messages and prayers they sent. As I tucked her in and was saying goodbye that evening, Linda looked at me contemplatively and said, "I didn't know I was making so much difference."

"Most of us never have that opportunity," I replied.

WE HAD A complicated plan worked out for that weekend which gave everyone some down time. I got to sleep a little later on Saturday morning and get some laundry done. The nurses' aides knew I wouldn't be there and would help Linda with her shower – something they did for most patients anyway, patients who weren't fortunate enough to have retired mothers around. Dave would go to therapy that morning and then bring Linda home.

That afternoon Dave and Linda had an appointment with Kathy, the realtor, to look at some houses. Even if they were unable to get out of the contract for the house that was being built, they had to find something that would be accessible for Linda. We joined them to provide a second opinion and to help keep an eye on Jared. He took care of himself by falling asleep in the car as soon as we left the house. So that we didn't exhaust Linda with houses that weren't even viable prospects, the plan was for Dave, Lamar and I to do a quick scouting of a house first. If we thought it was something Linda might want to see, we would bring her in from the car to see it. I'm sure this must have seemed strange to the homeowners who were home while we toured.

We did take Linda into one house that afternoon but the house needed a lot of work and was a far cry from the new house they had been building. An unspoken question was how much should they sacrifice what they wanted in a house for the need to be on one floor. Kathy had warned that ranch-style houses were in big demand now as the area's population was aging and new homes were mostly two-stories.

On Sunday morning we went to the hospital so I could help Linda with a shower. We spent a leisurely, relaxed morning. Connie and later, Gretchen, another teacher who was on a child rearing leave, Dave and Jared joined us.

Lamar and I soon left for home, taking Jared with us for some good "grandma and grandpa" time. We did all the things he has on his "list" to do when he comes to our house – play with his trucks in the mulch, ride on the ATV, have a Jacuzzi bath and make cookies. Such a long time had passed since we'd had any quality time with him. Our energies and time were so focused on Linda.

As I filled the tub for his bath that evening, Jared was bouncing around in typical four-year-old fashion and noticed his photo on the cover of a little jewelry box I have in the bathroom. This little box, made with his mother's help, had been his Mother's Day gift to me the year before. "That's a picture of me in the spring," he proclaimed. "That picture was taken when I still had a mommy."

"You still have a mommy," I said.

"No, I don't! No, I don't!" Jared taunted me much as he might another child his age.

I reached for him and sat down on the side of the tub, lifting him onto my lap. "You still have a mommy and she loves you very, very much!" I gave him a big, reassuring hug and tried to hide my tears.

By the time his bath was ready, he had already forgotten his comment. But I certainly couldn't. As I read him stories that evening and tucked him in, I wished we could somehow wave a magic wand and return to life the way it had been before the surgery.

February 12

MONDAY SEEMED LIKE a new beginning. Dave came for morning therapy and with the news that the builder had sold their new house the first weekend it was on the market. This resolved the financial problem, but there were still some tears of disappointment for what was not to be.

After lunch, for the first time since she'd been in the hospital, Linda put on make-up *and* wore her wig. We followed this major accomplishment with a grand tour past the rehab nurses' station, then up to the ninth floor where she'd spent her first ten days in the hospital, then on to therapy. Everyone agreed she looked beautiful – and so did I.

All this was in preparation for the visit from her students after school. We'd put the word out via a "mom" phone chain that they could come between 4:00 and 5:30 p.m. And come they did – fifteen of her nineteen students and, later in the evening, some former students as well. One student, Robert, even took time from his eleventh birthday to come. The kids brought cards and happy faces; we served cookies and punch. Several moms came, too. Linda showed the students how she was remembering them through the "student of the day" posters. She was so overwhelmed by their visit she couldn't talk much, but shed many happy tears. So did we and so did the rehab staff who stopped in to see the kids or peaked in the doorway.

That evening, Linda received a very special message from a former Mason Ridge student who was now a junior in high

Then the students had their turn to visit .

Enthusiastic hugs and a chance to read Linda's scrapbook of cards and letters from students. Robert even came for his 11th birthday.

school. I remembered seeing her when I occasionally went to Linda's school to help out. She was not in Linda's class but had "adopted" her, frequently volunteering to help with her class. Her poem says it all.

My Hero

I am here to speak today,
Of all the times you've passed my way,
The smiles you shared, the laughter you spread,
The lessons you taught and the values you instilled.
From morning to dusk from the first words of the day,
We knew you would always be there,
You were there to stay.
School wasn't a chore,
No, it was fun now,
To see a fun loving woman who was willing to enjoy,
There was this way about her that brought people together,
A way that I will always remember.
The days passed by and my school days with you ended…
that was not the end,
No, I had more unfinished business needing attention.
Seeing the baby, helping with your room,
Those were all decoys, so that I could be with you.
Having fun times as I saw the world in a new view.
Listening to your jokes, and listening to Patty say, "Don't smoke,"
Made my day so much brighter, made my soul so much lighter.
My incoming teachers, boy were they in for the worst,
They couldn't believe what I was under,
THE SPELL
The spell of happiness, joy and free will.
The spell of values and lessons that you had instilled,
The spell I could never hide from, neither want to nor need to.
The spell you put upon me by treating me as an equal person.
You may not have been my classroom teacher,
But to me you were more. You were my confidante, my preacher.
Today as you live and all revolve around you
It is time that you know just how much
I LOVE YOU!

Laura Liberman

THE NEXT DAY I went to Jefferson City for the Missouri NEA lobby day. It was the first day in six weeks that I had not spent at least some time with Linda. While it felt good to have a brief respite in the real and normal world, I felt guilty just the same.

When I arrived at St. Luke's the following day, Linda greeted me cheerfully, proud that she had showered and dressed herself with little assistance from the aide. I teased her about putting me out of a job, but she reached out for a hug.

"I missed you," she said.

As with any parent/child relationship, there are peaks and valleys. In Linda's and my case, these had been smoothed out as she became an adult, a wife and then a mother. Sharing the joys of these experiences had made us very good friends. These six weeks had intensified that friendship. Out of necessity, perhaps, we had developed the ability to communicate both thoughts and emotions without words. As I watched this beautiful young woman who was my daughter struggle with this horrible illness, I was so proud of her courage, spirit and determination. I told her one evening that regardless of the outcome, I would always remember this as a very special time. Linda agreed.

Linda's spirit and determination had made her a favorite in the rehab department. She was an inspiration to the other patients there, many of whom had significantly better odds at returning to a normal life than she did. One man in particular was giving the therapists a very difficult time, cursing and belligerent and refusing to try even the simplest tasks. One or two of the therapists had refused to work with him any longer – an option they have when the patient is totally uncooperative. As we were waiting for Linda's turn for therapy one day, he was being particularly loud-mouthed and irritable.

"It's hell to get old," he said.

Looking him straight in the eye, Linda said, "I'd sure like the opportunity."

ONE PERSON WHO had the opportunity to live a long life was my mother, Linda's grandmother. Although she had been living in assisted living for four years and had some serious health problems, at 89 she was still a prolific reader and kept up-to-date on world events by watching CNN and C-SPAN. When I would call her to give her an update on Linda's condition (she was not twenty-first century enough to have e-mail) she would often say, "It's just not fair. It should be my turn."

My mother almost got her turn while Linda was in the hospital. Our phone rang very early one morning at a time when we were already on edge for any calls coming at an unusual hour. It was the nurse from the residence where my mother lived. My mother had had a mild heart attack and was being sent to a local hospital. Under normal circumstances I would have rushed to catch the first plane to Syracuse. Now, though, my place was with Linda and I obviously couldn't travel. I put some of her friends in touch with her and called the hospital two or three times a day. I did the best I could. I felt torn, sometimes, for my mother insisted that she didn't need to be in the hospital anymore – she wanted to go back to her room at the home. I think her real fear was that she would have to go to a nursing home. The hospital wanted to send her to a rehab facility where she could receive more intensive physical therapy. I tried to assure my mother that the rehab visit was recommended so that she *could* go home – just like Linda. She was still suspicious.

After what seemed like an extremely long delay waiting for placement, I finally received a call from the new rehab center where she was to stay for a week or two. (All our communication was via cell phones and voice mail.) The young-sounding man who called, began by asking if I knew anything about rehab services. I assured him that I did – Linda was in speech therapy when I took the call. Somehow I thought this gave even more significant meaning to the phrase, "the generation in the middle."

February 17

NOW THAT DAVE and Linda were out of the contract for the new home they had been building, they were free to look for something else. Although Linda continued to do well with climbing stairs in therapy, she was far from being able to climb stairs independently. Even if the dining room of their home had been temporarily converted to a bedroom, the only full baths were on the second floor. A one floor plan would be much easier for her to navigate. Dave's parents, Rick and Rachel, had come for the weekend to see Linda and help with the house hunting. We had a wedding to attend so this also gave them some time without this set of in-laws around.

Dave called Saturday afternoon to report that Linda had climbed the stairs at home to take a nap but they both had found negotiating the stairs very difficult. The good news was that they had found a house. We joined them the next day to take a look at the house ourselves and to provide another opinion.

The house was on a corner lot in a lovely older neighborhood with tree-lined streets and much larger yards than are available with new homes now. The location was ideal – less than a mile from Dave's work, close to Jared's future school and within an easy drive to Linda's school – and St. Luke's Hospital. Although the house was thirty years old, it had been well maintained. Most importantly, even though we hoped it would be a temporary necessity, the floor plan would work for someone confined to a wheelchair. A large, combination living-dining-kitchen area meant that Linda could always be part of the action even though moving from one area to another was difficult. A large front room, used as a family room by the former residents, could easily be used as a dining room. The hallways were wide enough and straight enough for her chair but the bathroom doors might need to be widened. That was something we could do. The house also had an amazing – and huge – completely finished basement with another bedroom and bath, wonderful storage including a cedar closet and plenty of play space for Jared.

"We'll take it," Dave and Linda told Kathy, the realtor.

With the decision made, we all went out for a family dinner to celebrate together. Jared was as bouncy as ever. Life was almost normal. Linda returned to the hospital that night, tired but in a good way. Each time she returned to the hospital from a day pass, the family and patient had to complete a report of activities.

"We bought a house," Linda told the nurses.

I suspect that was the first time that "house-buying" had been listed as a day pass event.

Perhaps buoyed by the prospect of the new home, Linda had a phenomenal day in therapy the next day. Rick and Rachel came for the morning session as she proudly demonstrated how much she had improved since their last trip. Connie joined us for a celebratory lunch in the hospital cafeteria. I sat in on speech therapy, something I only did occasionally. Linda was not only reading sentences; she was reading short paragraphs, something she could not have done even a few days before. That afternoon, as Trish was doing leg exercises with her in physical therapy, she told Linda that her goal was for Linda to be able to walk with a cane when she left the hospital.

Without hesitation, Linda replied, "My goal is to walk!"

MASON RIDGE IS located on a heavily traveled road that happens to be close to St. Luke's. Shortly after the announcement each year, the custom is to post the name of the "Teacher of the Year" on the sign in front of the school. I decided that it would be wonderful if Linda could get a special noontime pass to see the sign and have her picture taken with her kids. Besides, there were a couple of students who hadn't been able to come to our little open house at the hospital, students Linda really wanted to see.

We obtained the necessary release from the hospital and drove the short distance to the school, arriving just at the end

Linda has a "day-pass" to visit her students and see the sign in her honor.

of the students' lunch period. Immediately, we faced some obstacles that I hadn't anticipated – mud and a curb that wasn't exactly wheelchair accessible. With some volunteer help, we managed, and the hugs and photos went on for almost half an hour.

During this process, Linda kept looking around. Someone was missing: Jesse. Jesse was a city student who was at Mason Ridge as part of the voluntary transfer program. He'd had lots of behavior problems before becoming part of Linda's class in fourth grade. Linda had a very positive effect on him. She'd found the "hook" that made him want to cooperate and learn. She had worried while she was in the hospital about how he might behave when she wasn't there. At the time of our visit Jesse was with a special learning group. No one had thought to include him. Because of Linda's insistence and obvious concern, someone was sent to get Jesse. Soon he joined us and the picture taking started anew.

Our noontime outing concluded with a trip to McDonald's for lunch. If it's possible to have a great day in a hospital, this day was one of those.

That evening Kathy brought the papers for their new house to the hospital for Linda and Dave to sign. Within a few days and a few counter-proposals later, the deal was closed.

Our spirits were high as I reported that evening.

Linda Update, February 23

Big news: It looks like Linda and Dave will be the proud owners of the ranch house they bid on this week. The anticipated moving date is late spring.

Better news: Linda will be getting out of the hospital on Friday, March 2, just in time for Jared's fourth birthday party on Sunday, March 4. (This is the family one; the kids one will be at Chuck E Cheese the following week.)

Best news: In physical therapy Linda was able to move the tendon muscles in her right foot and to curl and lift up her toes for the first time. She can walk with a cane now, with minimal assistance. She even got in trouble with her nurse yesterday for getting in the shower by herself. There is always the danger of falling but sometimes it's the little things that we can do that mean a lot!

Martha

OUTSIDE OF SPEECH therapy we were also seeing significant improvement. Linda was definitely able to ask questions now and could also express her opinions. This helped us finish a formidable task – completing her application for the district "Teacher of the Year" selection. Debbie and the other teachers on the selection committee were quite aware that Linda might not be able to do this now. And that was all right. They still believed that Linda had earned the school "Teacher of the Year" designation, even if she didn't want to compete at the district level.

Linda was not about to let her school down. She wanted to make the effort even though she knew how difficult it would be. With only a little over a week before the deadline, Debbie brought the application form. She had completed the nomination section:

Linda Favero is a remarkable person. She gives all of herself to her students without any need of public recognition. When a child is put into Linda's classroom, that child becomes "hers." She will work hard to find success with that child. Linda believes strongly in building relationships. She has a keen sense of understanding about what makes kids tick, and she works through that avenue. Linda is always the first one to bring up how programs or events might affect the child from the city, or the child with little financial resources, or the child who just has different needs. She is an advocate for students, with the strong belief that there is good in each student but sometimes you really have to look deeply. She always finds it. Linda earns the respect and admiration of her students quickly and easily. Although at times she can be very strict, the kids know she cares and that she is fair.

One of Linda's passions is the environment and the balance of nature. In order to give her students authentic opportunities to witness that balance of nature, she takes her fifth graders to Forest Park on a monthly basis. Each student has adopted his or her own tree. Linda also takes her students on a zoo overnight. To make sure everyone can come, she keeps the kids who wouldn't have transportation with her until the program begins, taking them to dinner and making them feel special. She asks the PTO to help defray the costs of those who cannot afford to go otherwise and is always willing to use her own resources without the child ever knowing. She has gone to dance recitals, ball games, and plays that her students are in as well.

Linda is down to earth, has no pretenses, and is a take charge person. There is no problem that is too big for Linda to solve. She has become our team's expert in figuring out schedules and technology. All we need to do is tell her what we want and she does the rest. She is an invaluable resource.

Linda gives herself to the district as well. She is our NEA representative and goes to all the meetings and conferences. She is on the Young Authors' Committee and many other district and school committees. Linda does all she does for kids and our school while being a wife and mother caring for a very active four-year-old. She is also battling brain cancer.

Linda has been fighting cancer for six years. In December, she found out it was back. She has undergone surgery and is now in a very aggressive chemotherapy program. You will never hear her complain or feel sorry for herself. She is determined to beat it and her focus is strong and positive. Our entire community has rallied behind her. All of the people who have come forward to tell her of their support are the greatest testimonial of all as to how many lives she has touched. Past students, past families, past colleagues, as well as the people she is currently working with are better people because of Linda Favero. This one young woman has made a difference and continues to make a difference. She is a role model and an inspiration to all who know her. I am proud to be her colleague and proud to call her my friend. You will not find a better candidate for Teacher of the Year.

NOW IT WAS up to Linda – with my help – to do the rest. Although Linda was able to read some now, she could not write or type or spell. I brought our laptop computer to the hospital and each evening for a week, we would sit and talk. It helped that I had been a teacher myself. It helped that I had been in her classroom many times, assisting at times, just visiting at others. Debbie and Linda's other teammates also helped by briefing me on some of Linda's strategies and practices that they had observed. Our in-hospital experience of "twenty questions" to help Linda communicate expanded elaborately now, helping us accomplish this formidable task.

We would sit and talk, question and answer, then I would enter what Linda said into the computer. Next I would read it back to her to verify that that's what she wanted to say and how she wanted to say it, trying as much as possible to use her words and thoughts and ideas – not mine. After a strenuous day of therapy, we would work in the evening, sometimes for as much as two or three hours until neither one of us could think clearly anymore. One day before the deadline, we finished and I hand-delivered the application.

While much of the application contains jargon and information more pertinent to educators, three sections focused on her philosophy of education, her background and her efforts to improve the community. Here, in Linda's own words as I transcribed them, she describes what it meant to her to be a teacher.

I am a teacher of children, not just curriculum. As a result, my goal is to teach the whole child in every area of his or her development. I believe children need structure and parameters. I believe they need the adults in their lives to be in charge and to guide them as well. In my classroom, I expect work to be completed on time and I expect the best each child has to offer. I keep track daily of which students need prompting and send weekly success cards home, listing any missing assignments. These are signed by both the student and the parent and returned.

I run a democratic classroom. We vote on the rules and norms of behavior expected and then I do expect the class to follow them. I find when kids have a voice in their lives, discipline usually takes care of itself. The kids also have a much better understanding of what is acceptable behavior and what is not. The kids, therefore, are very good about correcting each other and even do so in an appropriate manner.

I love what I do, and therefore, I use a lot of humor in the classroom. The children know very early on that I am tough, yet fair, because I believe in them. I build classroom community through class meetings and day-to-day teach-able moments. When nec-

Mason Ridge teacher

essary and appropriate, I will be a strong advocate for any of my students. I will also be there to redirect them when needed.

I believe we must have high expectations for all students. We must win our students' trust and confidence and let them know what we expect. During the past two years I have "looped" which meant that I followed my fourth graders into fifth grade. I have one student in particular who would have failed miserably if I had not set high expectations for him. We met at the beginning of the fourth grade because I knew he had had problems in the earlier grades. I simply told him, "We can have a very good two years or a very bad two years. The choice is yours." He made the right choice and has made remarkable improvement. My confidence, trust and expectations for him have made a difference. So has "looping", because we have had two years to know and understand each other better. And yes, so has having a smaller class – only nineteen this year – made a difference because I've been able to give him more of the individual attention he needs. The weekly success cards have also made a difference, giving his parents regular feedback when he has met expectations and when he has not. This student is just one, excellent example as to why we, as teachers, should never give up on any student.

Good rapport with parents is another key to my achieving success with the kids. I am in constant contact with them, in person, by phone or by letter.

Teachers' workshop and a winning smile!

Parents feel welcome in my classroom. I encourage them to come to school and to volunteer in many capacities. We are on a first name basis by open house and I feel comfortable calling them and asking them for help at any time. They also feel comfortable coming to me with any issue, great or small.

I am a team player and I love working with other teachers. I learn so much from others and hopefully, they learn from me, too. I have the reputation of being able to put anything down in a schedule. Our school focus this year has been on long term planning. I developed a way to have a monthly calendar with each subject's "through lines" included on the same page to put in our planners. I enjoy contributing to the school as a whole.

I am proud to be a teacher. To me, there is no nobler profession than teaching. I am grateful for the opportunity to teach and know I am making a difference.

I am a product of the Parkway Schools, having attended all thirteen of my pre-college years in Parkway. Following graduation from Parkway West, I went to Illinois Wesleyan University in Bloomington, Illinois. I later completed my Master's at Maryville University.

Education has always been a priority with my family. It was assumed from my earliest years that I would go on to college. My interest in becoming a teacher was a natural because my mother was also a teacher. I remember helping her with projects for her classroom and serving as her "guinea pig" a few times when she was completing her graduate work. She always cautioned me, however, to become a teacher only if it was what I truly wanted rather than simply because she was a teacher. My grandmother also influenced my decision. She is a strong person with a genuine interest in people – a woman who completed college long before it was the norm for women to go on to higher education. She taught me the importance of being a life-long learner. Following retirement, she taught in an adult literacy program. More recently, my mother-in-law and sister-in-law, both of whom are educators, provided inspiration.

The decision to become a teacher was also influenced by the many wonderful teachers I had during my years in Parkway. I especially remember Elaine Gabler and Betty Spath, teachers who encouraged me at Claymont Elementary. I remember Marcia Moskowitz, my English teacher at Parkway West, who demanded nothing but the best from me, and Erik

Hagen at Parkway West, who was one of my favorite teachers and allowed me the opportunity to go on the week-long "close-up" trip to Washington, D.C.

I have always enjoyed working with young children. During my Parkway school years I was able to serve as a high school counselor for sixth grade camp and worked for three years as a student aide with the Parkway Summer Essentials Program. Being a part of the Parkway West Academic Decathlon Team also helped confirm my desire to teach.

My professional development has been greatly influenced by my teaching experiences before I became a full-time Parkway teacher. My first teaching job was fifth grade in Harvey, Illinois, an urban suburb southeast of Chicago. I understand what it's like to teach thirty at-risk kids with extremely limited resources and little parental support – not because they aren't interested but because they are simply trying to survive. The following year I returned to Parkway because my future husband had found a job in St. Louis. Due to the scarcity of open elementary teaching positions at the time, I worked as a substitute for a full semester and also taught summer school. This gave me experience in every elementary grade level and even in the specialty area of art.

Working with Dr. Mary Ellen Finch at Maryville University, workshops offered through Parkway, and post-graduate courses with Richard Overfelt have continued my professional development.

My personal efforts to improve the community have already been mentioned in this document. They include participation in the Forest Park Forever Partnership Project and the recycling effort at my school. My recognition as Missouri D.A.R.E. Teacher of the Year is testimony to the emphasis I place on this program. I believe that this program will make a difference in our future by improving the choices my students will make in theirs.

My time to do more outside of teaching and other school related activities is limited. Since I have been in

Parkway, I have been busy completing my Master's and continuing in post-graduate work. I also have a very active four-year-old. Adding to the complexity of my life is the fact that I have lived with a brain tumor for the past six years. One of the lessons I am proudest of teaching my students is that people can be cancer survivors.

February 23-March 2

LINDA'S LAST WEEK IN the hospital was devoted to getting ready to go home. This seems strange in this era, when most patients are discharged from a hospital in one or two days, but necessary in the case of rehab patients. Surgically, Linda could have been released after ten days, but at that time she couldn't walk, talk, or even feed or dress herself. Her road to recovery would have been much longer without the intensive therapy she received in rehab.

On Friday, the emphasis in physical therapy shifted to going up stairs with only a cane to assist her – not hand-railings. Dave, Lamar and I all participated in these sessions so we could help at home. Trish volunteered her own time to come to the house over the weekend to help with the stairs. Barb came, too, to offer suggestions on the placement of grab bars. Since the house would be put on the market almost immediately, the goal was to do the minimum – just enough to let Linda get by until the moving date.

On Saturday, Linda had a day pass so that she, Dave and Jared would have time together to concentrate on the adjustments they would have to make when she was released from the hospital. On Sunday, Lamar and I joined them so we could be there when the realtor came to list their home and make her recommendations as to what needed to be done in preparation for showing the house for sale. Fortunately, other than some touch up paint and cosmetic fixes, not too much needed to be done.

Transition therapy continued during the last five days. Brenda worked on "cooking" and fun, as we made tin can ice cream together. She also took us to the hospital gift shop, where Linda and I had been many times before. This time, the goal was for Linda to read price tags, communicate with the sales clerks and pay for items herself. Barb spent time with Linda in the rehab kitchen, showing her ways to move around the kitchen safely and still let her cook for her family. In physical therapy, Linda now worked almost exclusively on climb-

Trish and Barb, therapists and friends.

ing the long flight of stairs between the first and second floor of the hospital rather than the short "practice" stairs in rehab.

Much of the week was celebratory. The first celebration was the most impromptu – and the most disastrous.

Jared's birthday was February 28. I knew he would receive special recognition at preschool and I also knew he had two parties planned – one with family on March 4, Linda's first weekend home, and a second the following week for the preschool clan. A birthday is a birthday and a very important event for a four-year-old. This grandma just had to do something to celebrate that day, while not detracting from the events to come.

I talked with Linda about what we might do and called Dave. Some parents were bringing in dinner that night for all of us and I suggested that, at the very least, I would like to have a small cake for Jared at the hospital. Dave and Linda agreed and I went to the local grocery store to pick up a cake. The real "Thomas the Train" cake that Jared and Dave had picked out would be for the Sunday party. I also alerted the rehab desk that we were planning this small party for the dayroom around dinnertime. That was how I discovered that another patient's family was also planning a party, this one for a grandson of a patient. The grandson, too, was celebrating his fourth birthday.

Sharing birthdays seemed like something that would be fun from an adult perspective, but not from a four-year-old's – particularly when our party was just supposed to be a token celebration and the other child's was his family's party. Even with that, it might have worked out. We were almost finished eating dinner and Jared had already blown out the candles of the little cake I had bought. He did look at it hesitantly, until we reassured him that his "Thomas" cake – and his presents – would be there this weekend.

That's when the other family arrived. It was just the other child's parents, and of course his grandmother who was the patient, but it was different in two significant respects. First, they had brought a cake. It wasn't just a small, inconsequential little cake, it was a "Thomas the Train" cake, not just even a flat sheet cake but a Thomas "model" in the form of the cake. Jared's eyes filled with tears, but the other family came to the rescue, offering to give Jared a piece of this incredible cake. In fact, the other child even conceded to sharing the front of the engine!

OK, we're past that hurdle, I thought. But then, they started opening presents. Lots of presents. I ran back to Linda's room and retrieved a new book from among the many gifts visitors had been bringing for him when they visited Linda, but it just didn't suffice.

"Where are my presents?" Jared asked with a quivering lower lip.

"You're going to have lots of presents this weekend at your party and next weekend at your Chuck E Cheese party."

"But this weekend won't be my birthday." And with that he began to cry, one tired little boy whose mother was very sick and might never be able to help plan birthday celebrations again. It was just too much. Dave whisked him off to home and to bed.

FORTUNATELY, THE NEXT two days – and Linda's last two in rehab – went much better. On Thursday, we brought in a big basket of fruit for the rehab staff. Without exception, they had been professional, wonderful and kind and had earned our respect and our appreciation.

That afternoon we had a surprise visitor – a surprise both for the hospital and for us. *The Cat in the Hat* came to wish Linda well. Yes, I do mean the Dr. Seuss' character in full regalia, a costume that stands well over six feet tall and is also very warm for "the cat." The Cat is part of NEA's Read Across

America campaign and happened to be in St. Louis that day, accompanied by Donna and Greg, MNEA president and vice-president respectively, and close personal friends. My retired NEA friend, Ruthanne, had been the Missouri "Cat" for the past two years, entertaining children throughout the state.

When this strange contingency arrived at the hospital, Ruthanne had donned the costume in a restroom and was then escorted to the elevators, heading for the eighth floor and Linda's room. The costume is so tall she had to duck to even get in the elevator and couldn't stand erect once she did. At every floor en route, startled people stared with good-humored amazement. When they finally arrived at the rehab floor, they discovered Linda was not in her room and had to return to the first floor physical therapy department where Linda was just completing one of her last therapy sessions. Both Lamar and I were with her that afternoon as she rounded the corner and saw this strange entourage. The Cat was an immediate hit in the therapy department and a fitting almost-last-day tribute to this teacher who had earned the respect and inspiration of the rehab staff.

We shared many hugs, laughs and tears. Everyone had a picture taken with The Cat.

AFTER THE CAT'S appearance, Linda's last day was almost anticlimactic. We had begun the process of dismantling the collection of cards, gifts and posters a few days before. Dave and Lamar had already taken much of these home. All that was left was a final day of therapy and a celebration lunch for the inpatient therapy staff. Our spirits were high as we shared the luncheon I had brought in and everyone wished us well. Even Dr. Rosenfeld took time from his busy schedule to join us.

Much to our surprise, the rehab staff also had a going away celebration that afternoon, complete with cake and a gift certificate to a local restaurant for Linda and Dave. Linda's final departure happened to coincide with the time when some of the ninth floor staff, where Linda had begun this journey, were getting off work. With their hugs and well wishes – plus the good will of what seemed to be the entire hospital staff – Linda was homeward bound at last.

Linda Update, March 4, Home at Last!

Yes, she made it! Friday was homecoming day after eight weeks in the hospital. While she will continue to receive therapy at home for a couple of weeks and then back at St. Luke's outpatient therapy facility later, she was certainly ready. She will miss the people, though. There were lots of happy tears, cards, cake and well-wishers seeing her off. Even two of her doctors took part – her radiation oncologist just stopped by for a visit Thursday evening and stayed for an hour. Not to be outdone, her neurologist joined us for the lunch we had brought in for the wonderful inpatient therapy staff.

St. Luke's West is rated as one of the top one hundred hospitals in the country – and we know the reasons why. It's the wonderful people, from the cafeteria help to the neurosurgeons.

Just because she's home, don't stop those prayers and positive thoughts! The second round of chemo starts on Monday with another MRI in about four weeks.

Martha

Chapter Five

Home At Last!

DIFFERENT PEOPLE DEAL WITH STRESS in different ways. My approach was to talk to the world. This resulted in astronomical cell-phone bills during this period, but it also led to the "Linda Updates" which became a form of therapy for me. Not that I ever told the whole story in the updates. Whether it was a mother's wishful thinking or an acute case of denial, I was convinced that Linda could and would recover.

Dave, on the other hand, tended to keep things more to himself, confiding only in family and a few close friends. Perhaps part of his reluctance to ask or accept help was pride or perhaps it was male independence. I know he felt and expressed a strong commitment to his responsibility to "take care of my family." Perhaps he felt a sense of guilt – as we all did at times – that somehow we had failed Linda. Why hadn't we reacted sooner to some of the signs we had noticed, but because of Linda's own optimism were reluctant to acknowledge?

As soon as the updates started, I would share them with Linda. In fact, many of those done while she was in the hospital were pounded out on the laptop computer while she rested. I printed out copies of each of them and placed them at the back of the album we had begun of letters and cards from students. The first few updates I e-mailed to Dave, but he told me, "I don't need them, I know what's going on."

As a result of our divergent approaches to stress, my friends and family were very familiar with Linda's situation while some of Dave and Linda's personal friends were not. Certainly the Parkway community and my "NEA family" knew what was happening. These people started sending the updates on to others, sometimes people I didn't even know. The prayers and positive thoughts that were received in return often helped give me the courage to keep going.

Although Linda had mentioned she was having surgery in her Christmas letter, it was with the same casual attitude we'd all had about her surgery at the time. She was going in for an operation. She would be in the hospital for a short while and then come home. Everything would soon be back to normal. For Dave and Linda's neighbors and friends who were neither teachers nor people they saw regularly before Linda went into the hospital, this scenario was all they knew. I discovered this the afternoon Linda arrived home.

March 2

WE LEFT THE hospital in two cars: Dave with Linda and me alone. Dave took Linda home and got her safely settled on the couch to take a much-needed nap. He then left to wrap things up at work and pick up the handful of prescriptions that Linda would need. I did a couple of errands, picked up Jared at preschool and went to their house. We tiptoed in so as not to disturb Mommy – something this rambunctious little boy was going to have to get accustomed to and live with.

I hadn't been there long when the doorbell rang. It was the neighbor across the street with her daughter, Kirstie, who was exactly the same age as Jared and a playmate of his. Kirstie had seen Dave getting Linda out of the car when they arrived – and the wheelchair. While the neighbors had known Linda had been in the hospital, they didn't know that she had been there that long or how serious it was. What a great resource of help and support they might have been to Dave had they only known!

Dave's parents and brother, Nick, arrived late that night. On Saturday morning, we all met at Linda and Dave's new house. Dave, Lamar and Rick went over every inch of the house, checking out things like plumbing and electrical and things the building inspector had noticed. I did a fast measuring job of all the rooms and windows. This was the one chance we had to get measurements before the April 1 closing date. We wanted to be ready to get to work as soon as the house was theirs. Rachel and Linda toured at a more leisurely pace and Jared explored his new yard.

Dave left while we were there to take Linda to the beauty salon for her first real haircut and manicure since going into the hospital. I was to pick Linda up shortly thereafter. When Dave realized that Linda didn't have any cash, he gave me his credit card. I kidded him about what I could charge now and tucked the credit card safely in my purse – or so I remembered.

When I arrived at the beauty shop only a few minutes later, I searched the car frantically but couldn't find the same credit card I had teased Dave about only minutes before. I soon gave up. I was embarrassed but it didn't really matter. Linda was so pleased to be part of the real world again. Dave was very nice about it and promptly cancelled the credit card. I did find the card in my car a few days later, but only after the cancellation process had been initiated.

The rest of the weekend was a flurry of activity as all hands pitched in to get their current house ready for sale. Things like touch-up paint, cleaning windows and dusting in those out-of-normal-cleaning places, were accomplished quickly with all hands on deck. The realtor's tour would be the following Tuesday and the house needed to be ready to show to prospective buyers.

First, there was a birthday party to attend to on Sunday afternoon – Jared's. This was the family gathering, with the Bierks included. And finally, Jared's own "Thomas-the-Train" cake and presents and pandemonium, all the things that make a four-year-old's party what it should be. The debacle of the hospital party was long forgotten.

Dave told me that Linda had been having some cramping pains in her right side since the evening before. She seemed uncomfortable that afternoon, but didn't complain too much. Was she just trying to hide her discomfort for the sake of the party?

Perhaps we'd just tried to do too much that weekend.

March 5

At 5:00 A.M. on Monday morning the phone rang. It was Dave calling from the emergency room at St. Luke's. During the night the pain in Linda's side had gotten worse and he'd finally taken her into the hospital. "There is no need to rush," he said. "We're just waiting for tests."

While I didn't exactly rush, I arrived at the hospital by 8:00 that morning. It was to be a long day full of tests, ruling out first one thing, then another. As a new medical record was quickly being gathered, we seemed to be repeating history. Couldn't they just retrieve the charts from her two-month stay that had just ended the Friday before? Why did we need to reinvent the wheel? Part of the problem was that Linda's primary doctors on the case, Dr. Cuevas and Dr. Rosenfeld, were not immediately available. Although their back-ups were familiar with Linda's case, they still weren't the main decision-makers. So we waited.

Rick and Rachel had gotten Jared ready for school and then joined us for part of the vigil before heading back home to Illinois late that morning. They left after a CAT scan had ruled out appendicitis. At 3:00 p.m. Linda was given a sonogram. The results wouldn't be available until the next morning. At 4:30 p.m., after more than twelve hours in the emergency room, Linda was readmitted to the hospital. This time we were sent to the surgical department on the seventh floor. "We're working our way down," I thought, "first the ninth, then the eighth, then the seventh . . ."

The new nurse was very reassuring and comforting. She gave Linda some powerful pain medicine that seemed to help. At least it knocked her out for awhile. Her new room seemed very bare and bleak after the color of all the cards and posters and flowers of her room on the eighth floor. I wanted to rush back to Linda's house and retrieve them but we all hoped this stay would be brief – just find the cause of the problem and fix it.

Tuesday was another long day of waiting. Dave took the morning shift with Lamar and I arriving about noon so he could go back to work. Linda had been awakened about 6:00 a.m.

for some pills but neither Dave nor Linda knew why. The results of the sonogram had not yet been reported. When I finally asked a nurse, she said the results of the sonogram had been normal, ruling out things like gall bladder and kidney problems. The doctors suspected that Linda had a blood clot in her right leg, something that is not uncommon when there is limited movement of a limb. They also felt that a piece of the clot may have "shot off" into her right lung. Another test was supposed to confirm or disprove this theory. At almost 3:00 that afternoon and another full day in the hospital, they came to get Linda for the "VQ" scan. The results would come back "tomorrow."

Meanwhile, word had gotten out to the hospital staff that Linda had been readmitted. I had called "Home Therapy" to tell them to delay coming so the rehab people knew. Word spread from there. With Dr. Rosenfeld's blessing, an order was written to resume in-patient therapy so Linda wouldn't lose all the progress she had made. Ironically, the same therapists who had worked almost daily with Linda for two months and had just discharged her on Friday with much fanfare, now had to do a "preliminary" evaluation before therapy could begin again. Hospital red tape!

I joked with Linda that you know you've been in the hospital too long when the volunteer receptionist at the information desk remembers your name and room number without having to look it up. You know you've been in the hospital too long when your mom is offered an employee discount from the cafeteria manager and the cleaning crew waves and asks how you're doing. You also know you've been in the hospital too long when the staff from other floors and departments come to visit you.

The good news was that none of the possible suspect diagnoses were any indication that Linda's brain tumor was spreading. In addition, while she was in the hospital she was being given a more powerful pain medication than she had at home. And, if a blood clot was the culprit, it could be relieved with a simple surgical procedure. And so we waited some more.

I ARRIVED AT the hospital early the next morning expecting to hear the results of the procedure done the afternoon before. Linda's nurse of the day was the same one that had been almost invisible the day before. She did make a brief appearance when someone else came in to take some blood samples. When I asked her for the test results, she said they were waiting to hear from the doctor and disappeared. A very nice young aide helped me get Linda into the shower. This shower was not as handicapped accessible as the one on the eighth floor had been, nor was the aide experienced with transfers, but somehow we managed. With Linda feeling cleaner and more refreshed, we settled back again to wait. Still no reports and still no nurse.

After lunch, as another day seemed to be fast escaping, I decided I had to do something. I made a quick trip around the department to see if I could find Linda's nurse. She was nowhere in sight so I left a message at the nurses' desk that we would like to speak with her. Meanwhile, I called Linda's doctor. "What? You haven't been told anything yet?" the voice on the other end of the line said. "Those results were in this morning. We'll send someone over right away."

About a half-hour later, Linda's nurse strolled into the room, smelling strongly of cigarettes. She settled herself comfortably in Linda's wheelchair, crossed her arms and said, "You wanted to see me?"

Both Linda and I were stunned.

I explained that we'd been waiting all day for the test results. I told her that I'd just spoken with Linda's doctor's office and learned that the results had been available all day. The nurse shrugged and said that she couldn't reveal test results – that was the doctor's responsibility. She also added that the resident doctor should have gone over the results with us that morning. After two months of only good experiences with St. Luke's staff, this nurse's lackadaisical attitude and apparent lack of any genuine concern were a shock.

Minutes later Dr. Cuevas' counterpart came and confirmed that Linda did indeed have a blood clot and gave the order for the necessary surgical procedure. His order was just in time as the latest this procedure could be done was 4:00 p.m. Linda was the last patient of the day. Fortunately, too, it was the very pleasant – and caring – evening nurse's job to escort us to the surgical floor and tend to Linda afterwards. As we wheeled down the hall, I told her about my frustration with the day nurse. She rolled her eyes, nodded her head and pointed toward the door of the head nurse where I reported our encounter with incompetence the next day. As I told the head nurse, it was a good thing I had had seven weeks of positive experiences by which to judge St. Luke's.

On Thursday, Linda was released from the hospital again with no pain and no limits on either her diet or her physical activity. The procedure had worked.

Linda was home again at last!

LINDA'S FIRST FULL week at home was a struggle for all of us as we tried to adjust and adapt to her current limitations after her long hospital stay. The first few days were especially challenging. Linda was weaker after her extra four days in the hospital. She also had to get used to maneuvering in a home that wasn't built with a handicapped individual in mind. The apraxia that still affected Linda's speech often affected her recall of the simplest tasks. Little things like putting on make-up, something that she was extraordinarily adept at normally, even left-handed, could be terribly frustrating.

We had to get used to letting Linda experience frustration so that she could relearn normal, daily tasks herself. Our tendency was to jump into action at her slightest move. If she stood up, we'd immediately ask, "What do you need?" or "What's wrong?" when perhaps all she wanted was a change of view. I remember her stopping in mid-step one time after I'd responded in this way. She shook her head and shook her hand (and cane) in frustration and in tears said, "It's hard to be loved so much!"

To complicate matters, Dave and Linda were trying to keep the house squeaky-clean and neat so it could be shown. To ease this situation, they spent much of the first couple of weekends with us. As to Jared, he was very glad to have his mommy home at last. The Chuck E Cheese birthday party, his official one for the four-year-old crowd, was a special treat for all of us.

We also had to learn what "home care" meant. While the three therapists who were working with Linda were all very nice and seemed to be professionally competent, they were used to working with people who were completely homebound. For most of their patients, it didn't really matter when they appeared but for Linda it did, at least if she was going to be able to do anything else other than therapy. At first the therapists insisted that Linda was supposed to be "homebound" in order for them to work with her. This was an insurance requirement, they said. We had been told that it would be only a week or two before Linda could return to outpatient therapy at St. Luke's. The home therapists insisted that they never worked less than three weeks with a patient. Too much paperwork was involved to do otherwise.

Fortunately, the "homebound" assumption proved to be incorrect and we were able to work out a schedule that suited everyone. She saw each therapist – speech, occupational and physical – twice a week for about an hour each time. Dave would help get Linda downstairs in the morning, get Jared ready for school and head for work. On the mornings when she had speech therapy, I would arrive a little later which gave me a chance to get a few things done at home. The other therapists came late in the day so Linda and I had the time in-between to go – and go we did, whenever she felt up to it.

Our first expedition was to the grocery store. We chose a Monday afternoon when the store would be less crowded. I went in first to check out the logistics and to find the motorized shopping cart. Since she didn't have a handicapped parking tag yet, it seemed easier to bring Linda into the store in her own wheelchair, then transfer her to the cart. That part worked fine. But the controls for the cart assumed that you were right-handed or that your right hand could at least function – which Linda's did not. She managed to wrap her left arm across the front of the cart and we made our somewhat jerky, stop-and-start way through the store. The aisles were wide in this particular store. This was a good thing, I suspect, for otherwise Linda might have careened into a shelf full of bottles.

Linda only had a few things she wanted to purchase and we actually found ourselves laughing out loud. "Student driver," we explained to other customers in the store. Later as we checked out, I didn't try to explain to the cashier at the checkout counter why Linda had only given her $20 for a bill that was quite a bit larger. Her concept of money, cost and change had been mostly erased by the apraxia.

Our next trip to a different grocery store was not as successful. The store was crowded with customers shopping for the weekend as it was Friday afternoon. The motorized shopping cart was different from the other one we had used and required some relearning to operate. Linda had walked (with her cane) too far from the car to the store and was tired before she began, compounding the problem. Once settled into the cart, she insisted that she would be all right on her own. She had a small list that she had painstakingly filled out on a computer form. Long before her recent hospital stay, she had devised this shopping list when writing by hand had become too difficult and time consuming.

I left her to her own resources while I did a little quick shopping of my own. When I found her a few minutes later, she was at one end of the dairy aisle, the cart pointed into the corner – and in tears. The controls of the cart had been just too complicated for her to manage. That was the second and last time she tried to use one of the electric carts. For subsequent trips, we used her personal wheelchair or one of the non-motorized chairs with a basket that some stores provided.

ANOTHER OF our early expeditions was to the mall to buy her some new clothes. Linda had grown understandably tired of the "sweats" that had been her outfit of the day while she was in rehab. Mall shopping was much easier, even though we discovered that the merchandise was so crowded together in many stores that it was difficult to maneuver our way through with the wheelchair. Manage we did, for Linda had not lost her exuberance for shopping, nor had I lost the spirit for shopping with my daughter.

Late in the afternoon after we returned home from this shopping trip, Linda received a phone call. I answered the phone and handed it to Linda. It was a member of the committee who would select the Parkway School District

Teacher of the Year. Linda was one of six elementary teachers who were finalists. The next step in the selection process were interviews that would be held the following week. Linda handed the phone to me to get the details. I had the unenviable task of explaining the situation and told the woman we would have to wait to see if Linda was up to it.

After the call, we talked about the interview. Did Linda want to go through with it? She was honored to have made the semi-finals but was realistically concerned that she might not be able to talk much in an interview situation. She did want to try, pending how well she was doing when the time came. We decided to practice some at home and while we were driving. I would pose possible questions and she would answer them. Even with this help, it was apparent that the interview would be a challenge.

I called team teaching partner, Debbie, and a member of the interview committee. She assured me that the committee was aware of Linda's situation. They had also agreed that she could share the questions with me if that would help. I thought it would. The evening before the interview I stayed over at Linda's, both to rehearse and to help her get ready the next morning. Her appointment was at 8:30 in the morning at the Instructional Services Center, a good half hour or more drive from Linda's home even under non-rush hour conditions. She was going to give it her best. She had the full support of her students who sent letters offering their suggestions for doing well in the interview – from a fifth grader's perspective.

Dear Mrs. Favero,

Congratulations! How have you been? We decided to come up with tips for the interview. First thing, be relaxed and say what first comes to your mind.

Whatever you do, do not eat hot dogs, beans and onions before the interview! They will cause bad effects. Have good eye contact. If you're staring down at your feet, they will think you don't want to be teacher of the year. Brush your teeth, dress nicely and have good posture. You don't want to look like a bum out there!

Eat lots of TicTacs.

Spencer

Dear Mrs. Favero:

Here are some helpful interview tips:

Do you remember that mom that walked by when you (joking) threatened to beat us? Well if she happens to be there pretend that you remember no such thing.

Good eye contact – don't wink at the interviewer.

Brush your teeth so you show off those pearly whites.

Don't eat onions – you'll be crying enough without them.

If they ask why you should be teacher of the year, here are some reasons in case you can't think of any:

You make learning fun.

You help us solve our problems by giving us a hug.

You are nice and don't let us misbehave.

You love teaching.

You love kids.

You make sure we know we can tell you anything.

You have been brave, hardworking, confident and an excellent role model.

We think you are the best teacher in the world and we love you.

Good luck on the interview and keep these tips in mind.

Love, Anna

Dear Mrs. Favero:

If they ask you why you think you deserve Parkway Teacher of the Year, here are some answers:

Kids can come to me about anything.

I love each child in my classroom.

I am a hard working teacher.

I am involved in educational issues.

I have a relationship with each child.

I am a fun teacher.

My kids enjoy how I teach.

I try to be a role model.

I am there for them and I can always know what's going on.

I am so excited for you! I know you will do what you are best at.

Crazy Kid #1 AKA Tracy

Dear Mrs. Favero:

Are you excited about your interview? Here are some tips for interviews. (Trust me! My mom gets interviewed all the time on the NEWS!!!)

You always want to make a good impression. Tomorrow, when they ask you why you think you should be a candidate, I think you should say, "Well, I'm a good teacher, I am loved by my family and students, and I am a good comedian." When they ask you how did you get so much confidence, I think you should say, "I always think of my students and my family."

Always smile and don't forget to brush your teeth and eat a Tic-Tac before you get interviewed. I miss you a lot and I hope I see you soon.

Alyssa

March 16

I'M NOT SURE what time Linda got up that morning but I know it was very early. She'd gotten dressed in one of her new outfits we'd purchased just the week before. Dave had helped her down the stairs and left for work. Instead of her rehab tennis shoes, she had on dress-flat shoes for the first time. She worked and worked on her make-up in the half-bath downstairs. Because she was nervous, it took longer than usual. The clock was ticking and I was beginning to pace.

Finally she was ready to go and she looked lovely. I helped her down the two steps into the garage, then left her for just a moment to go back into the house to get my purse. She walked to the car with her cane. Then, rather than waiting for me to help, decided to get in the car on her own. I came to the open kitchen door just in time to see her lose her balance, the slick-soled shoes betraying her as she glided down the side of the front seat and onto the damp garage floor. Other than her dignity, she wasn't hurt.

We now had a real dilemma. Linda was far too heavy for me to lift from the floor and she still had no strength in her right leg or right arm. Someone was watching over us at that minute, for as I was trying to figure out what to do, a neighbor came by, saw our predicament and offered to help. He got Linda off the floor, we brushed off her clothes which weren't in too much disarray from the mishap, and off we went.

By now it was raining and we were running late. Traffic was horrible, as it always is on a rainy day. We finally arrived at the Instructional Services Center with just minutes to spare. It was pouring. Umbrellas are hard to manage with a wheelchair. If I tried to hold the umbrella, I couldn't push the chair. If Linda held the umbrella, I couldn't see where we were going. We both were a little wet but finally made it inside. Now the question was where to go in this maze-like building that was definitely built prior to laws requiring handicapped accessibility. I searched the building to find the committee and discovered there was no way to get Linda to the room where they were to meet. The committee graciously agreed to come meet us.

So late, wet and with a slightly damaged ego, Linda faced the interview committee. We sat at the top of a short flight of carpeted stairs with the committee gathered below us. The first question came. Linda got as far as, "I believe that . . ." then faltered unable to continue. She was trying desperately to hold back the tears.

Stress and apraxia had kicked in. I reached over to hold her hand. The committee asked the next question with the same result. Debbie finally came to the rescue and began to fill in for her, saying that if Linda could answer, here's what she'd probably say. As I recall, they even let me help some. I will always remember and appreciate their compassion and understanding.

When we left the building, Linda burst into tears. "Don't worry, Hon," I said. "The committee was impressed that you were even there."

I was right. I later learned that she had come in third, even though she couldn't answer even one of the interview questions for herself.

THAT SAME AFTERNOON we made a special trip to St. Luke's for Linda had developed a strange rash that itched terribly. We had called the kind and good-humored dermatologist, Dr. Muccini, who had seen her for a different rash while she was in the hospital. The return phone call came while Linda was working with the physical therapist, who was pregnant. From my description over the phone, the nurse thought it was probably shingles and warned that exposure to shingles can be dangerous for pregnant women – not to them, but to the unborn child. The therapist finished that session but another physical therapist was sent the next time until Linda's expectant therapist could check with her doctor and until Linda had visited the dermatologist.

I wasn't sure Dr. Muccini recognized Linda at first, but I was mistaken. After a quick examination – and another prescription – he confirmed that it was shingles but had been caught early and should dry up very quickly with an antiviral. Then he added what we both were thinking, "You don't need this, too."

A follow-up visit two weeks later showed that the shingles had all but disappeared. He wished Linda the best of luck and as he did so, we both noticed he was trying hard to keep his composure – something I had never seen a doctor struggle with before. At an appointment some time later when I was the patient, he apologized to me for his seeming lack of control. This caring physician had previously been a neurosurgeon but found he couldn't handle the emotional stress of seeing people just like Linda and, I suppose, feeling helpless about making them better. Shingles and acne can be cured!

ON SUNDAY, WHEN Lamar and I arrived at the house, I noticed immediately that the wheelchair was out in the garage. "Why? Is Linda sleeping?" I wondered.

To our amazement when we stepped inside, Linda was at the sink helping to make sandwiches. For most of the weekend she'd been relying just on her cane and had even been able to walk short distances without it, bracing herself when necessary on anything nearby. She confided to me that when she returned to outpatient therapy, she wanted to be able to show Trish she could walk without a cane.

That evening, however, "walking" did not go as well. We had all gone out for a light supper together before we headed home. Linda had insisted that she didn't need to have her wheelchair in the restaurant. She'd just use her cane. Getting her to the table was not a problem, but after dinner she needed to use the restroom. While Dave went out to warm up the car, I went with her to the restroom. Although she could walk with a cane, she still needed help sitting and standing, particularly in unfamiliar situations.

It was a long, slow walk. As we returned from the restroom and headed toward the front door, Linda was holding back the tears because she was in so much pain. I wished we had brought the wheelchair inside since everyone else was already outside waiting for us. The booths in the restaurant were all filled so there wasn't a place she could easily sit and rest while I went to get help. Through sheer determination, Linda finally made it outside and into the car.

The next day, Monday, the pain seemed to have dissipated. With a full schedule of doctor's appointments planned for Tuesday, we decided just to wait and see.

March 20

THE ST. LUKE'S Cancer Care center is a bright and cheerful place, probably designed that way to help spur the optimism of the critically ill patients who are treated there. The recliner chairs where patients receive chemo are in a large room with an institutional-size bay window. This glass wall allows plenty of light into the room and affords a view of a park-like area of the hospital grounds. Snacks and coffee are always available for patients and their caretakers. There is ample reading material – and blankets if needed – for those patients who have to sit a long time while the chemicals infiltrate their systems.

To paraphrase something my mother used to say about her assisted living residence, "If you had to go to a place like this, it was a nice place to be."

Linda only had chemo intravenously a few times for most of her treatments were oral medications. These treatments have the same effect – fatigue, nausea and weight gain. Linda never had much nausea but she did tire easily and had gained weight due to both the chemo and the steroids she was on to help reduce the possibility of seizures. Once a week she visited the Cancer Center for a blood test to make sure her counts weren't getting too low. The staff always seemed genuinely glad to see us and treated Linda with the utmost consideration and respect. Once or twice a month, these visits included a visit with Dr. Cuevas, the chemo-oncologist who was managing her therapy.

On this first visit since Linda had left the hospital, Dr. Cuevas was pleased with the progress and scheduled the second round of the chemo. He said we should wait until at least the end of April to have another MRI in order to give the chemo a chance to work – three full months from the last MRI in January. The end of April seemed like an eternity!

Dr. Cuevas could not explain why Linda was still getting the pain in her right side but he did not think it was chemo or tumor related. (Although the pain was intermittent, it was excruciating when it came.) He sent us to see the radiologist who had done the surgical procedure for the pulmonary edema – the blood clot detected earlier. An exam and an ultrasound said everything was normal and, in fact, the clot had already begun to shrink.

From there we went to Dr. Fischer, the rehab doctor. He, too, was pleased with Linda's progress and agreed to schedule Linda for outpatient therapy beginning the following week. As Linda had requested, rehab was stretching the rules a little so that both Trish and Lynn, the physical and speech therapists who had seen Linda as an inpatient, could continue. For occupational therapy, she would have a new therapist, Laura, one that Barb had highly recommended.

Dr. Fischer also repeated the suggestion that had been made when Linda left the hospital, to have "Lifeline" hooked up. This we did later that same week. Linda chuckled at the thought, mocking the television commercials showing an elderly woman on the floor saying, "Help, I've fallen and can't get up!" It seemed strange to have something like Lifeline necessary for someone as young and strongly independent as Linda, but this would allow us to leave her alone more. All she would have to do to get help when she was by herself was to push a button on a necklace. Lifeline would then call Dave at work, or us, or a succession of other numbers until help was reached. The same gadget could be used to answer phone calls when she was unable to get to a phone. Since she still had problems dialing phone numbers – and talking when under stress – Lifeline would give Dave and me much greater peace of mind. With Lifeline installed and outpatient therapy scheduled to begin, life would get easier, we thought.

Linda still had that excruciating pain, however, so we called the doctor again. An MRI of her hip was scheduled for that Friday. Linda had endured thirty-something MRIs of her brain but this was the first one on her hip. The results of this MRI confirmed that everything was normal. The doctors thought it was probably just nerves acting up as a result of the filter procedure to prevent the clots from going to her lungs. In time it would go away completely.

MY FATHER CAME for a short visit early the following week. He was en route home from a bridge tournament in Kansas City. (Yes, at 89, he was still playing championship flight tournament bridge and hadn't missed a national tournament in over thirty years.) The visit gave him a chance to see his only granddaughter, Linda, and his great-grandson. It also let him know, better than I had ever wanted to tell him by phone, just how serious Linda's condition was. Even though he was able to spend a day or two with us, I don't think the seriousness of Linda's illness registered.

Linda didn't feel well during his visit, either. Whether it was from anxiety or reality, she felt she was regressing in both speech and walking. She was also very tired – probably from the chemo. At her request and because of my concern, we

scheduled an extra appointment with Dr. Cuevas. He agreed
to schedule the MRI a little earlier – April 10 instead of at the
end of the month. He warned that this was a compromise. It
still might be too early to tell how effective the chemo had
been.

THANK HEAVEN FOR the buying and selling of houses! There
was so much to do to get ready for the move that it kept us
from dwelling on that next, critical MRI.

Dave and Linda had decided to leave the kitchen and the
front room (which they planned to use as a large dining room)
as they were for now. Relatively new Berber carpeting in most
of the house and wood flooring in the kitchen would also stay
intact. The family room desperately needed to be stripped of
metallic silver and mauve wallpaper and the small kitchen
pantry was a hodgepodge of underused space. New, white six-
paneled doors and light fixtures throughout, and new plate
glass mirrors in the bathrooms would help update the house
that had been built in the early '70s. The bedrooms and
bathrooms needed new paint or wallpaper just to make it feel
like their house instead of someone else's.

Moving to a new house gave Linda and me all the excuse
we needed to shop – something we had always enjoyed doing
together. In between home therapy visits, doctors' appointments and when she felt up to it, that is exactly what we did.
With the floor plan I had drawn up of the new house and measurements in hand, we picked out paint and wallpaper and
window treatments and some things just for fun.

We were quickly indoctrinated into the logistical challenges
of shopping with a wheelchair and a cane: narrow passageways
to navigate, bumps in pavement and finding a way to carry
the purchases we'd made. As I commented to Linda, I had
always thought handicapped parking spaces were close to the
stores. I no longer felt that way as I ran packages out to the car
and then returned to get Linda.

When we happened to be in the area, we often drove by
the new house to refresh our memories and our excitement so

that reality could sink in. On one such drive-by, the owners were loading things into a truck in the driveway. Linda motioned to me to stop and the owner came over. Linda reached out with her left hand to shake hands, introduced herself as the new owner and said how much she was looking forward to moving in. She was speaking with relative ease and she didn't have to get out of the car. I'm sure the owner never knew or suspected the "rest of the story."

Closing was scheduled for April 2 and, in just two short weeks, we were ready. In the meantime, Dave and Linda had been successful in finding a buyer for their current home. That closing date was set for April 25 and another hurdle would be out of the way. With the house sold, packing could begin. Everyone pitched in – teachers, friends and family, with Linda doing what she could. Of course, she had "packed" and organized much of the basement over the Christmas holidays, getting ready, she thought for the other house they were going to buy. What providence!

Rick and Rachel came to help that weekend and, on Saturday, we all went on the "walk-through" of the new house. It was on that visit to the house that the move finally hit home with Jared and he asked which room would be his. When Linda showed him his future bedroom, he reacted immediately.

"Oh, no! I don't want *flowers*!"

We assured him that the truck wallpaper border he helped pick out would be in place before he moved in. That seemed to satisfy him and he went outside to explore his new yard.

April 2

THE CLOSING ON the house went without a hitch. Fortunately, Dave had had power of attorney for a long time so could sign for both Linda and himself. But Linda was there, dressed-up and as excited as any new homeowner would be.

I joined them at the end of the closing and later Lamar came, too. Together, we all went through the house one more time, now that it was actually theirs, making notes of things that we needed to bring and setting priorities for things to do. Our goal was to get as much of the work done as possible before they moved in, tentatively scheduled for the fourteenth of April.

Fortunately, this was just the kind of work that Lamar and I both liked to do and we'd had plenty of experience. Lamar was an electrician by trade and could also do plumbing. During our early marriage years, he'd painted apartments in our complex for extra income. Our first house was a fixer-upper. That's when I learned how to wallpaper. Our second house was new, but Lamar had done the electrical work and we'd done all the interior and exterior painting to save money. Our third house was at "The Lake," on property purchased before Linda was born and while the lake was still a field. When Linda was in elementary school, we'd designed and built – literally – a vacation house. Later we'd expanded and remodeled the same house into a home for permanent living, the one in which we still live.

Lamar was chief contractor on this new project. He always had difficulty being a hospital visitor or even a well-patient visitor, but this project gave him something tangible he could do. Within a few days he painted the ceilings throughout the house and most of the interior walls. Without hesitation, he knocked out walls, rebuilt doorways and added grab-bars to make the house more wheelchair accessible. He was getting this house ready for his little girl.

I was chief caretaker, at least during the day. When I wasn't helping Linda or taking her to therapy, I was the wallpaper hanger.

Dave was chief husband, daddy and "bring-home-the-the-bacon-guy," doing what he could on weekends and evenings. Dave would take Jared to school and then bring Linda to the new house on his way to work, saving us some driving time. Linda's major job was to get better – and to help us when she felt up to it and could.

Friends Nancy and Jack Bierk, who had helped us with many of our earlier projects and who were also retired, would help, too, particularly with stripping wallpaper and painting. Ed, a retired industrial arts teacher, assumed the task of redoing the kitchen pantry and making the wood floor match where the pantry doors were to be widened.

Rick and Rachel came on the weekends when they could but Rick still had to be careful because of his own recent surgery. Rick and Dave concentrated on the remodeling of the hall bath, getting the new doors ready and removing overgrown shrubs. They also used Rick's truck to start the moving process from one house to the other.

Rachel helped me – and Linda, as she was able – to strip wallpaper and do some of those cleaning jobs that need to be done before you move in. Teacher friends pitched in, too, when they weren't busy teaching or with their own families and obligations. The adage that "many hands make light work" certainly applied in this case.

Jared's room was the first room completed. After all, we had to get rid of those "flowers." The upper half of the room was painted white, the lower half a deep blue. The wide "truck" wallpaper border he had helped select encircled the room at chair-rail height. The room had two closets – one for clothes and one with new wire shelves for toys. It looked just like a four-year-old boy's room should look.

Jared was thrilled when he saw it completed for the first time. He would proudly show "his" room to anyone who would accompany him to look. One of his first visitors was the principal of the school he would attend when he entered kindergarten. The principal, a former colleague of mine and someone who had known Linda as a little girl, stopped by to say hello when she saw the bevy of activity at the house. When she left after a brief visit, Jared asked, "Where did the 'president' go?"

Each day we made progress. The master bedroom was painted and wallpapering was finished. We were simply waiting for the new kingsize bed to be delivered to complete the project with the new bedspread, valences and pillows. Eventually, Linda and Dave planned to completely redo the master bathroom. For now, the sink was accessible and a wall was knocked out to make the shower and toilet accessible as well.

The guest bedroom was not a priority as far as necessity was concerned, but it was for Linda as a matter of choice. She was decorating this room exactly as she had planned for the other house. The walls were painted a pale sky-blue. A wide picket-fence wallpaper border she had seen in a display home went around the base of the room. The wallpaper, complete with cottage garden flowers, and the new blue and white checkered comforter and valences were charming.

When the guest room was all but complete, she motioned me off to the other end of the house while she had Dave search packing boxes to find the afghan I had cross-stitched for Jared's christening. The afghan featured the fourteen angels and the opening lines from the song from *Hansel and Gretel*. I had often sung this to Linda as a baby and toddler. We never did know all the words but improvised. Although I hadn't been aware of it, Linda had a friend sew special hangers on the afghan to make it easier to use as a wall hanging. Soon she called me back to see the results. Hanging from a rod over the bed, the afghan was the perfect finishing touch.

Linda's young friends who stopped by to visit and see the house couldn't believe what we had accomplished in such a short time. One friend said, "You've done more here in two weeks than we've been able to do to our house in over a year."

It does help when you have a lot of experienced retirees as volunteers.

LINDA'S PROGRESS WAS not as encouraging. Within a few days of closing, she had a seizure. It occurred in the morning as she, Dave and Jared were getting ready for the day and while we were driving in to meet them at the new house. As Dave explained to me by cell phone, Linda was walking from the kitchen to the living room when her leg started shaking. He'd gotten her to the couch as quickly as possible, but not before Jared observed a seizure for the first time. It only lasted for four or five minutes, but was scary just the same. Although we had been warned that more seizures were a possibility, this was the first one she'd had since January.

When we arrived at the new house, I raced inside to put together a makeshift bed for Linda in the front room. The ceiling in this room had been painted and no other work was necessary prior to the move. The room had become the temporary resting place for paint cans, light fixtures and tools as well as items that had already been moved from the other house. Fortunately, the mattress and box springs from the guest bedroom and some sheets and blankets were already there.

With the bed ready, I went out to meet the car as Dave and Linda pulled into the driveway. I still remember the look on Linda's face when we first made eye contact. It was a look of sheer terror – and genuine discouragement.

We cancelled therapy for the day and Linda spent most of the morning sleeping in the front room while Lamar and I worked in the back part of the house.

Although the seizure had not lasted long, it did seem to have a significant impact on both speech and walking. This was a morale crusher, making Linda very frustrated that she couldn't do more. Two days later, on Friday, she went to outpatient therapy, still tired from the seizure. This was also the first time she had been scheduled with Trish. Her goal of showing Trish that she could walk without a cane was not possible now, even though she had been able to do so at home the week before. Now she could barely complete one lap around the therapy center with her cane before collapsing exhausted in her chair. The new occupational therapist, Laura, had noticed a positive difference in the movement of her right arm, though. Linda was able to tell the difference, too. She needed that.

The next MRI was only a few days away. We waited.

Linda Update, April 9

'TIS THE NIGHT before Linda's MRI – over two months since the last one and we're all holding our breath. Dr. Cuevas, the chemo oncologist has warned that this MRI may not show what we want because it hasn't been long enough for the chemo to take effect and do it's thing. If that's the case, he'll order another MRI in the near future. In any event, for everyone's peace of mind, especially Linda's, we need to see what's happening.

Keep those prayers coming – we still have a long way to go!

Martha

Linda Update, April 10

ONCE YOU'VE BEEN on the "waiting end" of waiting for MRI reports for over thirty times – or is it thirty-five now? – you know that the longer you wait between the MRI and the report, the worse the results are going to be. Today's wait was about an hour and a half. The news could have been worse but it also could have been much better.

The good news is that the front tumor has shrunk slightly. This is the tumor that was "debulked" with surgery in early January. The middle tumor, the one that was diagnosed six years ago, appears to be stable.

And now for the however. The tumor towards the back of the brain has grown about thirty per cent. Of equal concern, this tumor is in the area that controls speech and vision. While Linda's vision does not seem to be significantly impaired, speech is still a struggle.

What next?

Tomorrow we meet with the neurologist and we may (or may not) learn more about the long-term impact of this new growth. Linda will also continue with speech, occupational and physical therapy, three times a week.

Linda completed the second round of PCV chemo today. Because of the tumor growth, her doctor feels the chemo routine needs to be changed. If approved by the insurance companies, she will begin taking thalidomide – a drug only recently approved for use in cancer patients. We don't know how long she will be on this drug but probably for "a long time" according to her doctor.

Meanwhile, life goes on. After our morning at the hospital, Dave and Linda went home so Linda could take a long spring nap. I joined Lamar at the new house where we're working as fast as we can to get the house ready for the move-in, scheduled to begin officially on Thursday evening.

Saturday I'm hoping to take Linda to the walkathon for cancer being held in her honor at Mason Ridge.

To all of you, please know that your thoughts and prayers are greatly appreciated by Linda and all of us.

Martha

April 11

WE NEVER MADE it to the neurologist's appointment the next day or to outpatient therapy either. Linda didn't even want to get up in the morning. Dave managed to help her downstairs and then called us.

Besides her fatigue, she was having extreme difficulty managing the stairs. According to her doctors, the dramatic change for the worse since yesterday could be depression, could be the tumor or could be the change in her medication. In all probability it was a combination of the three. Her medications were adjusted and she was being given morphine for the pain. The morphine, of course, would just make her sleep more.

We decided to officially move Linda into the new house that day, even though the house wasn't quite ready. It would be easier for everyone. The makeshift bed was moved from the front room to the master bedroom even though it would be replaced with the new bed the next day. Dave brought Linda over and she spent most of the day sleeping while Lamar and I scurried around to put the finishing touches on the bedrooms, especially Jared's. He was ecstatic when he saw his new "truck" room finished and waiting for him.

Friends pitched in, too, and teachers joined them after school to bring clothes from the old house to the new.

Three days earlier than anticipated, Dave, Linda and Jared moved in unceremoniously and spent the first night in their new house.

Linda was home at last!

Chapter Six

Spring

WHAT A DIFFERENCE A DAY makes! Linda's headache finally went away this morning. Friend Gretchen stopped by with her two kids about 10:00 this morning. She helped feed Linda some jello and we finally saw Linda's pretty smile again. She was able to get up, take a shower and she was actually hungry for some lunch. Her timing was perfect for the new king-size bed was delivered at just about the same time. We were able to get it assembled before she needed a nap again.

But she did rejoin us a few more times during the day and was up and about when Dave and some of his co-workers arrived with the furniture.

While I'd like to give Gretchen full credit, increasing some of Linda's steroid medication apparently did the trick. This had been gradually reduced during the past three weeks in an attempt to get her off steroids and some of their unpleasant side effects. I think Linda would rather tolerate weight gain and some facial hair than have the headache and nausea for one more day.

Meanwhile, progress on the house continues.

Martha

April 14

IT WAS A beautiful Saturday, cool in the morning but gradually warming up and getting quite warm by midday. The weather was perfect for the Walkathon for Cancer at Mason Ridge Elementary School.

The event was the brainchild of five fifth grade girls. At a slumber party in January the girls had talked about how much they missed Mrs. Favero and what they might do to help. Their vision was simple: pick a Saturday and have fifth graders come to walk laps around the school track for a penny per lap. There were no pledges and no special tracking system to determine how much money was raised. The girls did most of the planning and work themselves, enlisting the help and support of their parents.

Dave and Jared took Linda to the site in the morning; I joined them shortly thereafter. Participants signed in at a table that had been set up for that purpose and also signed a gigantic six-foot "Get Well" card. The crowd was small at first but soon began to grow. Fifth graders and first graders and whole families came to show their support. Teachers and parents and former students came as well. Each walker wanted to greet Linda and give her a hug to wish her well.

Linda was in tears most of the time, overwhelmed by the response. Teaching partner Debbie wheeled Linda around the track and so she made her laps, too, accompanied by students and other teachers. It was hard to determine how much money was being collected because most people simply made donations, then did laps just for the exercise.

This beautiful day also happened to be the day before Easter. KSDK News Channel 5, the NBC affiliate in St. Louis, was looking for feature stories that day and had heard about the event. The camera crew sent out to take some footage was impressed. They wanted to know how long the walkathon would continue – it was now about 11:00 a.m. – for they wanted to send a reporter and make the walkathon the feature story for the evening news. The reporter couldn't get there for another hour or so. Would there still be people?

Parents spread the word and people lingered and stayed. When the reporter came some walked laps all over again –

*Linda and the organizers of the
Walkathon for Cancer*

Linda and Martha

The Walkathon for Cancer raised over $7,000!

some had walked continuously. Parents and students and former students and family were interviewed. The reporter asked if he could interview Linda. Dave did check with her but she declined. She was too emotional by the turnout and, besides, speech difficulties would have been just too apparent. It didn't matter. The tape that aired on all three newscasts that evening and the next morning as well, told the story. Kids were shown hugging Linda and walking laps while voice-overs by some students told how much this teacher meant to them. A few fifth graders stayed long enough to read some of the letters they had written that had been collected in the scrapbook, retrieved from Linda's house amidst the unpacking. The lead-in to the news commented about one teacher and her students who were making a difference.

The kids raised over $1000 that day with much more to come in the following weeks – ultimately over $7000. What a wonderful tribute to Linda and what a positive learning experience for the kids!

SATURDAY WAS ALSO moving and unpacking day. Moving is stressful enough even under normal conditions but factor in a critically ill wife and mother, a walkathon for cancer in her honor, plus television coverage and that stress multiplies.

When I finally returned to the house that afternoon, things were pretty chaotic. Linda was napping, exhausted from the morning. People seemed to be everywhere. Ed and Lamar had just discovered that the new doors for the redesigned kitchen pantry had been cut too short and would have to be revised. That meant unpacking the kitchen, the project planned for the afternoon, would have to be delayed.

I was excited about the television coverage and wanted to make sure the VCR was hooked up by the 5:00 o'clock news. The reporter had warned me that if we didn't tape the event then, we might have difficulty obtaining a copy later. Getting the VCR operational definitely wasn't a priority for anyone else. Dave left to mow the lawn at the other house, taking Jared with him. That house was still being shown pending the

Linda, Dave and Jared at the Walkathon

Linda and her students—celebrating the moment!

approval of the contract. "Did the lawn really need to be mown that day?" I thought to myself.

Shortly after Dave left, Debbie, her daughter, Nicky, and my friend, Jan, came to help. Linda was still napping. Dave had specifically asked that we wait until Linda could help to unpack the things for the china cabinet. The kitchen was on hold so I decided that we might be able to make a dent in the shambles that was now the basement. Jared had immediately dumped all the plastic bins in which his toys were stored as soon as they had arrived. These were strewn from one end to the other of the large recreation room. I was also anxious to get the guest bedroom downstairs set up. I had spent one night in the beautifully redecorated guest bedroom upstairs but it still didn't have doors. Besides, Dave and Linda needed some privacy and "together" time with all the helpers that were coming in and out of the house.

At the very least, I thought we could get the downstairs bedroom set up so I could use it and so it would be available for Dave's parents who were coming for the week. We quickly went to work. Jan helped me set up the bedroom. Debbie vacuumed. Nicky helped sort the toys into their appropriate bins. We were almost finished when Dave came home.

Stress! Dave came down the stairs and yelled in frustration for us to stop, saying he wouldn't be able to find anything. "Every time I come home," he shouted, "the whole goddamn NEA is here!"

He then went outside to mow the lawn. It was his therapy.

Those of us working in the basement were stunned – and I was embarrassed for my friends and Linda's. I found Dave outside, furiously pacing back and forth, mowing the lawn in the process.

"I'm not mad," he said, yet still sounding quite mad. "Stressed" is probably a better term for how he – or anyone in his situation – might feel.

I reminded Dave that although many of the people who had been pitching in to help happened to be NEA members, that was irrelevant. More to the point, these people were my friends and Linda's friends, too. That was especially true of the people there that afternoon. Jan had known Linda since she was in kindergarten. She and her brother had even joined us on a canoe trip through the Minnesota boundary waters. Debbie was Linda's teaching partner and Nicky was there because she adored Jared.

Dave's reaction did cause us to slow down. It really didn't matter. The house was more than livable by now. Besides, the "goddamn NEA" continued to help. That same afternoon after Linda got up from her nap, Jan helped her unpack the china cabinet. Although Linda needed help with the unwrapping, she could and did have very definite ideas about where she wanted things to go.

ON FRIDAY, PASTOR Amy, Linda's high-school-friend-now-minister stopped by for a visit. She was so wonderful and encouraging with Linda. She presented her with a beautiful, hand-knit purple prayer shawl that had been done by the women of the church – with a prayer for every stitch. When she reminded us about the beautiful services held on Easter at Manchester Methodist, we had said we would try to be there.

Easter Sunday was another spectacular morning. When I arrived at the house to help Linda get ready, she was still in bed. She got up to use the bathroom and wash her face but that took all the energy she had. I helped her back in bed and said I would go to the Easter Service for both of us. For months I had been holding back the tears in front of Linda, trying to camouflage them with optimism. But as I tucked her in and gave her a hug, I broke down.

"I'm sorry," I cried, "but it just kills me to see you like this!" She returned my hug and patted my back with her good left arm, the patient comforting the caregiver.

Standing out in front of the church dressed in a white ministerial robe, Amy glowed as she greeted people as they arrived. When she saw me coming alone, she didn't have to ask. She embraced me as I explained, "Linda was too sick to come so I came for both of us."

The church was crowded as it always is on Easter Sunday, particularly at the main service when the choir sings Handel's *Messiah*. I found a seat very close to the front of the church.

Suddenly, I felt overwhelmed. Perhaps it was the contrast of the beautiful sanctuary filled with Easter lilies with the darkened bedroom where Linda was resting. More likely, it was just the strain of the past few months. The tears that had started in Linda's room returned. I think I cried, silently, through most of the service and was grateful that I had a good supply of tissue.

If I had to pinpoint a time when my grieving process began, Easter Sunday was probably the moment. But when I left the service I felt a little more ready to face the challenges that lay ahead – at least for awhile.

As I'm sure every cancer patient's family knows, when you have someone who's being treated and the treatment doesn't seem to be working, people come out of the woodwork to let you know about new treatments that they've heard mentioned. "Have you gotten a second opinion?" they ask, or "Have you heard about this?"

With the help of the Internet now available, you can investigate them all. You have nothing to lose. I was beginning to sound too much like a medical expert myself, which I'm definitely not. I just wanted to help my daughter survive. At some point, though, I think you just have to trust in your doctors and in God to know what the best course of action is.

A new drug was featured on a prime-time news story about this time. I didn't see the show because I wasn't watching much television these days, although I certainly did hear about it. This drug, at the time still called STI 571 because it was so new, had been found to treat leukemia successfully. It was still in clinical trials for brain tumors. We were experienced with clinical trials. Linda had been part of a Phase III clinical trial for Temodar, another chemotherapy, two years before when it was discovered that her tumor might still be growing after radiation.

Following her surgery in January, I had contacted a clinical trial experimenting with an advanced laser surgery, but Linda's tumor was too large for her to be included in that particular study. Even if we could find a clinical trial for her, Dave was adamant that he didn't want Linda to be a "guinea pig." He also didn't want her to have to leave home – a requirement for most Phase I and Phase II clinical trials. I couldn't disagree with that.

On hearing about STI 571, I contacted the Dana Farber Cancer Research Center in Boston where one of the trials was being conducted. Since my brother lived just outside of Boston, it seemed like a possibility and the Center has an excellent reputation. The research assistant who took the information sounded quite positive at first about Linda's fitting the eligibility requirements. Then I learned that for any of these studies, the patient needs to be pretty self-sufficient, for they have to live on site. That ruled Linda out.

The assistant reaffirmed what Linda's own Dr. Cuevas had said, that no evidence was available to indicate that STI 571 had any effect on brain tumors.

We could have pursued other second opinions but that would only have delayed treatment. It was Linda's choice to go ahead with thalidomide, the drug Dr. Cuevas was recommending. A recent study had shown that thalidomide, used in conjunction with the potent chemo, BCNU, had shown positive response in tumors of her type.

Because of the horrible effects this drug had on babies in the 1950s, lots of red tape is required to obtain a prescription, and it is very expensive. A two-week supply can cost $2000. First we had to get the insurance approval, which we did, thankful that Linda had good medical insurance. Then the doctor, the patient and even the pharmacist must fill out forms for the agency that monitors the use of thalidomide. The agency is extremely diligent in their mission. Even after you've been cleared to take the medicine, forms have to be filled out weekly verifying that you are not pregnant. Miss sending in one form and the agency is on the phone to find out why.

Linda started on a dosage of 800 mg that was gradually increased to 1000 mg per day. That meant swallowing sixteen to twenty huge pills, the size of vitamin supplements, every night. Tapioca and ice cream helped. With the first few doses she had the expected nausea, but soon got over that. She was also having painful tumor headaches. Morphine helped these but also zapped her energy.

The most frustrating part, for Linda and for all of us, was the continuing deterioration of her speech. The cause for the regression couldn't be determined. It could be medication, it could be the seizure, it could be swelling putting pressure on the speech center of the brain, or it could be the tumor itself.

We'd just have to wait until the next MRI, scheduled for sometime in June.

THE HOUSE WAS quickly getting settled, thanks to the help of so many friends and Rick and Rachel, who came for a week. Linda, too, was able to pitch in, particularly in setting up and organizing the kitchen for when she would be able to return to what once had been favorite pastimes, cooking and baking.

We soon settled into somewhat of a routine. Outpatient therapy dominated a major part of that routine. Three half-hour sessions, three times a week, should have been just a small part of the day. We'd thought they could be scheduled back-to-back and they were once we got a routine established. The rehab-scheduler and the therapists themselves really worked with us on that.

Rarely, did we leave the hospital in less than two hours, and the sessions were exhausting. They were exhausting for Linda – she was the one getting the therapy, but therapy days were exhausting for me as well. They were physically exhausting because of the energy and strength it took to help Linda down stairs, up stairs, into the car, out of the car, into the restroom, out of the restroom, up the elevator, down the elevator, from one hospital building to another. They were emotionally exhausting because I was watching the suffering – and pure grit and determination – of my only child.

Dave would take Linda to therapy about once a week or when I had another obligation so that he could observe her progress and learn how to help at home. Sometimes Lamar, Nancy and Rick and Rachel would help out as well. But still, whenever I could be there, I couldn't relinquish this self-imposed assignment to anyone else. They could join us and keep us company, but I felt I *had* to be there.

Strange as it may seem, our visits to therapy and the hospital were rewarding and sometimes even fun! We'd laugh and cry and we'd go to the now familiar hospital cafeteria where many of the staff who knew us would come over and see how Linda was doing. One day a nurse who had given Linda some specialized x-rays when she had the blood clot in her leg greeted us in the cafeteria. She helped Linda to a table while I got food for her. She told us, "You're the kind of person that makes people glad they're in this profession. This is why we do what we do."

On nice days, we often ate lunch on the patio outside the hospital cafeteria. Linda would lean back in her wheelchair to face the sun and soak up the rays. Or we'd just sit and relax and enjoy watching the geese that gathered around the hospital pond. We even tried going for a walk around the hospital jogging track, but pushing the wheelchair up the hill to return to the hospital took all my strength.

We also began trying to leave Linda at home by herself a little more, at least in the morning before therapy. With Lifeline installed and Dave working nearby, this plan was feasible. Linda was relieved to have some time just to herself and that gave me a little more time at home as well. The first morning that I purposely arrived at 9:30, just in time to leave for therapy, she was dressed and waiting. Dave had helped her some before he left for work. The rest she had done on her own.

"How did it feel to be by yourself?"

"Ahhhhhh . . . . wonderful!" she sighed.

But we were still spending too much time at St. Luke's. Monday, Wednesday and Friday became therapy days. These days often stretched into four-to-five-hour days by the time we got home, for we often included lunch or stopped somewhere afterwards. We would arrive home just in time to take a nap. Tuesdays were doctors' appointment days and sometimes Thursdays were as well.

Weekends were family time or sometimes simply a time for Dave and Linda and Jared to be together.

April 25

THERAPY WAS NOT our only activity. Linda still had more recognition events for being named her school's Teacher of the

Year. The first of these was a special Board of Education meeting where all the honorees were recognized. Families were invited as well. Dave decided to stay home with Jared – he would go to the Appreciation Dinner with Linda the following week. So Nancy joined me in taking Linda to the Board meeting.

Less than an hour before we were supposed to leave, I wasn't even sure Linda would be able to get out of bed. But she did manage to get up, get dressed and even put on some make-up, camouflaging how she was really feeling.

Have you ever been guilty of thinking that there are just way too many handicapped parking spaces? I had – before we needed them. The three handicapped accessible parking places were already in use when we arrived at the junior high where the meeting was being held. (Two of the cars did not have the appropriate handicap tags.) Nancy helped take Linda into the building while I found a place to park.

Once inside, both Linda and I attracted a lot of attention. Many, many people came over to give us their best wishes. We sat in the front row, not because we wanted to be conspicuous but because it was the easiest place to maneuver the wheelchair. An assistant superintendent in charge of the selection committee read a brief statement about each of the candidates, following which each proceeded through a short receiving line, shaking hands first with the superintendent, then with each of the seven Board members.

Even though Linda was not the "District Teacher of the Year" or even the "Elementary Teacher of the Year," the presentation to her was slightly different from the others. The assistant superintendent's voice cracked as she shared some of Linda's accomplishments as a teacher. These were the reasons her colleagues had named her "Mason Ridge Teacher of the Year." She was then wheeled through the line by her mother – me. The superintendent shook Linda's hand as he had with the other candidates. The Board president, however, gave Linda a warm hug. One by one the other Board members followed suit although a couple of the men weren't really sure whether they should shake her hand or give her a hug, so did both. For the group picture, Linda was in the front row.

The evening was memorable and I was so glad that Linda had been able to go.

As word spread about Linda's Teacher of the Year recognition – and of her illness – letters and cards from former students continued.

Dear Mrs. Favero:

I have been waiting a couple of years now to tell you something that is very important to me for you to know. When I was in your class, you touched me like no one else could. I felt like an individual among my peers and I know they did as well. What was most important, though, is that you gave me a sense of passion.

I missed you so much in middle school and then came to the realization that there would never be another teacher like you. Middle school brought a lot of new things into my life. It helped me to know that I wanted something that you had. I realized that I wanted nothing more than to be exactly like you – I wanted to be a teacher. I want to do everything you did for me for others. I have never been more inspired and I thank you for helping me recognize my dream and all my goals in life.

You have touched an incredible amount of people. People who don't even know you and hear of your story are inspired. You are a true fighter and the most courageous woman I've ever met.

You mean a lot to this community and to Mason Ridge families, especially mine. We think about you constantly and you are always in our hearts and minds. Kristen and I will never forget what you did for us, how you changed our lives and so many others.

I know you have many students and some of them may be too young to realize it now but you are truly a gift to the educational world.

Words cannot describe the amount of inspiration you have provided for all of us.

Love always, Katelyn

Dear Mrs. Favero:

Hi! This is Lindsay. I heard that you weren't feeling so great so I decided to write this letter on a pink piece of paper. Pink always makes me feel better so maybe it might do the same for you!

I just wanted to tell you that all of the lessons you've taught me have really paid off. Last year in English we learned a lot of vocabulary words. I was thrilled that I knew almost all of them. I knew these words from your spelling tests.

When you were my fifth grade teacher, we listed admired traits and qualities of each other. I still have my sheet. Whenever I'm feeling down I read it and I feel better. Thank you for that little piece of paper that has turned many of my bad days into great ones. . .

I just want to thank you for being my teacher. You have made a difference in my life not only with your lessons about school subjects but with your lessons about life.

Love, Lindsay

Mrs. Favero:

I'll always remember you as the best teacher anyone could ever have. I want to thank you for not just teaching me my school lessons but life lessons. You have enriched my life. I'll always love you.

Brooke

April 28

SINCE FEBRUARY, WE had been planning to attend the musical *Aida*, playing at the Fox Theatre. I had had season tickets for the Fox the past few years, which I shared with Linda. Neither of our spouses were real theatre buffs, so the Saturday matinees had become our special outing. We often joined my "PNEA gang," my name for a group of close teacher-NEA friends, for lunch. They also had season tickets to the Saturday matinees. The past few performances I had given my tickets to other friends.

On Valentine's Day, Dave wanted to give Linda something special. Her room was already filled with flowers – including roses from him in recognition of her "Teacher of the Year" status. He suggested, instead, that they both go to *Aida* after she was out of the hospital. It was a wonderful idea and gave her something to look forward to.

As a season subscriber, I had gotten the tickets and requested the special wheelchair seating she would need. I had asked my friend and theatre fan, Sandy, to join us on that day to use my "extra" ticket. Grandpa was the designated babysitter for Jared. He had gone in before me to finish up some of the detail work that still remained on the house. Sandy and I came later, laden with the carry-in lunch she had graciously offered to provide before we left for the theatre.

Unfortunately, just before Sandy and I arrived, Jared had behaved – or rather misbehaved – just like a four-year-old. He had been playing with water and buckets behind the house when Dave, dressed and ready to go to the theatre, came outside. From inside where he was working, Grandpa saw it coming but was helpless to say anything to prevent it. Jared grabbed the hose he had been playing with and sprayed his father. Not a good thing! Grandpa laughed. Also not a good thing!

Dave fumed, grabbed Jared, shut off the water and carried him inside. In the process he added mud to the mixture, both on the clothes he was wearing and to the Berber carpeting.

Sandy and I arrived to find an irate Dave, a still somewhat amused-but-shouldn't-have-been Grandpa, and a repentant-but-still-unhappy Jared. And, of course an upset Linda who really couldn't talk well enough to calm Dave, chastise her father or reprimand Jared. This was not exactly the formula for a pleasant lunchtime gathering.

Somehow, we managed to get through lunch. Dave was still stoically silent on the way to the theatre. At the intermission, Sandy and I joined the PNEA gang who were visiting with Linda and Dave in the special seating area for wheelchairs. Dave had begun to relax and I know he enjoyed the show.

That evening Lamar and I took Jared home to catch up on grandparenting and to give Dave and Linda some quality time alone together.

ALTHOUGH WE WERE spending a lot of time at St. Luke's, therapy was not going well. Laura, the delightful new occupational therapist, continued to see progress with movement in the right arm. This improvement continued to give us hope. The same was not true for walking. Linda seemed to be regressing, something that could certainly be explained by the powerful medications she was taking. She relied on the wheelchair most of the time. It was also becoming increasingly difficult for her to manage the two short steps from the house to the garage. Lamar had installed a handrail and a grab bar. These helped but going down these two stairs was still a slow and difficult process.

One morning as we were leaving for therapy, Linda lost her footing, slid down the doorjamb, catching my hand in-between. She landed on the bottom step. In the process, she accidentally hit the Lifeline button, activating the microphone in the family room.

"Linda, are you there, are you OK?" squawked the speaker box in the family room.

While she couldn't get close enough to call out an answer, I could and rushed in to ask them to call Dave. He wasn't immediately available so Nancy was called as the next person on the list – since I was already with Linda. By the time she arrived, we were laughing about the silly little accident. It could have been much worse. With Nancy's help, we were able to get Linda up again and into the car and off to therapy. However, this fall seemed to end her confidence in walking with a cane. She relied much more on the wheelchair thereafter.

A few days later, Lamar installed a ramp to go from the house to the garage so we wouldn't have to use the stairs again. I really had to "put on the brakes" when wheeling Linda down the ramp and it took all my strength to push her back up. The ramp was an improvement, however, easier – and safer – than helping her with the stairs.

About this time we discovered that Linda was having double or blurred vision. It didn't occur all the time, but the eyestrain added to her fatigue. That week we added a visit to an opthamologist to the list of doctors' appointments. The apraxia made it very difficult to get an accurate reading, because it can cause you to respond the opposite of what you really mean and because Linda did not consistently know the names of the letters. With me at her side to help interpret her responses, and using symbols instead of letters, the doctor concluded that her visual acuity was normal. The double and blurred vision were probably a result of medication or the tumor, not an "eye" problem per se.

Both Dr. Cuevas and Dr. Rosenfeld continued to think that the chemo regime was on track. Linda, herself, told me she did not feel like the tumor was growing.

WHEN LINDA WAS tired or anxious, her speech suffered. Although spontaneous language was still there at times, even that wasn't consistent. Most of the time she could talk on the phone and we kidded her about that. Driving home from therapy one day, I remember her smiling and saying, "I like my new neighborhood." I also remember her telling me at lunch one day, "I was just thinking, we haven't had an argument." She was referring to the fact that we were spending so much time together we were bound to have disagreements. But that hadn't happened.

These examples of speech were the exception rather than the norm. She could respond by nodding. Given sufficient time to frame her thoughts, she could talk some and answer questions but it was becoming more challenging for her, not less. Reading was also becoming increasingly difficult, but it was hard to tell if vision or apraxia was the cause.

Linda's speech therapist recommended support services from the St. Louis Wellness Community and "Talking Books for the Blind."

The Wellness Community facility in St. Louis gives you a sense of ease when you walk in. The décor is subdued but both cheerful and restful. On a hot spring day, the cool of the air conditioning adds to the feeling. On our first trip, we attended a relaxation group. We were the first to arrive and had to wait for the other participants as well as the facilitator. There was little small talk as we waited. I'm sure each of us was reflecting on why we were there and what it would mean.

The relaxation exercises came first, followed by an opportunity to share stories. We listened to one or two of the others. One was a young woman there to offer her mother support; another was a middle-aged woman well on her way to beating the odds against breast cancer. When it was Linda's turn, she tried to say a few words, faltered and looked in my direction. I asked if she wanted me to share her story and she nodded. Somehow I got through it, but not without grabbing for the handy box of tissue that was supplied.

After the session, we browsed through their library and checked out some books and videos that seemed like they might be helpful. We also made an appointment to return for the pre-counseling that was part of their program before being assigned to a regular support group.

When we arrived for that appointment we had not one, but two, counselors. Our counselor was being evaluated that day and her supervisor was there to observe her – with our permission, of course. As teachers, both Linda and I were accustomed to this practice and readily agreed. I was certain that this counselor would have an extra challenge. I was reasonably sure that most of her clients could talk.

We were given a brief introduction to the process – first we would each complete a questionnaire; then we would be interviewed separately. This was done primarily to determine if we were both genuinely interested and committed to the support group concept and if the group would be beneficial for us. The counselor assured me that they would help Linda with the written questionnaire and then escorted me into another room while they met with Linda. I completed my questionnaire and waited, not knowing how much or if Linda would be able to tell them about what she was feeling.

When they came to me, they certainly understood that Linda had brain cancer, which affected her speech, and that she was a very remarkable young woman. They then asked me to share what I knew. I had barely begun when everything I had been holding back, my hopes, my fears, my stress, caught up with me. I couldn't stop the tears. I continued, knowing that these people had probably seen this reaction many times before.

Finally, the supervisor said, "I need to caution you. The support groups we offer may not be what you're looking for. Most of our support groups are for spouses dealing with the illness of a spouse or a child coping with the illness of a parent. You're dealing with something quite different."

I had regained my composure by the time I was reunited with Linda. I don't think I ever told her how upset I had been, but I'm sure she knew. I did mention that the supervisor thought the support group might not be what we were looking for. We had thought the group might meet during the daytime for this retired mother and her very ill daughter, but all the regular groups met in the evenings. Why hadn't we thought of that? Of course the sessions would be held in the evenings, so that working spouses could attend, but somehow I had envisioned daytime groups as well.

We signed up for a group anyway but later cancelled. With all the therapy, life was too scheduled anyway. We both felt we might be better off just having some free time to "smell the roses." In fact, one day we did just that, taking a trip to the Missouri Botanical Gardens, one of my favorite places. The Gardens were also a reminder of more pleasant times. Linda and I had taken Jared there as an infant, just before she was to return to school from maternity leave. I still remember introducing him to the marvelous spring aroma of peonies.

TALKING BOOKS FOR the Blind was the other suggestion that we tried to follow. We were both pleased and amazed to find that Missouri – and I believe most states – have a wonderful service for people who are blind or suffer a neurological impairment that makes it impossible to read. Dr. Fischer, Linda's rehab physician had to complete a referral form for the state library. Next, we were assigned a staff person who would help select books that matched Linda's interests. We were sent lengthy catalogs, but the staff person would also regularly select books to send based on an interest preference list that Linda completed. Included in this free service was a special tape recorder with green "start" and red "stop" buttons.

Linda loved books, especially children's books, and had always read to Jared. Since her surgery, she hadn't been able to do that. I know this was one of her greatest disappointments – and terribly discouraging. Even when she had regained some reading skills, she still didn't attempt it. I don't think she wanted to frighten Jared, or perhaps she was a little embarrassed that even children's books were hard for her. So we ordered children's books on tape, too. That seemed like the perfect solution.

The books and the machine arrived, postage free. We were both eager to try them, believing that would be an easy way for her to do something she loved rather than just sitting or watching television. This, too, proved to be frustrating. Whether it was from neurological damage or because of the fatigue resulting from all the heavy medications, she had difficulty concentrating well enough to follow a story for long. She made a few attempts but soon gave up, finding that even the red and green operational buttons were difficult for her to operate. Whether she and Dave tried them when I wasn't there, I really don't know. I do know that the tapes kept coming until I called the library and said not to send any more.

For the rest of the summer the ones we had already received sat in a basket, but I don't think they were ever used.

TRUE TO OUR fashion of trying to make a bright spot out of everything we did, Linda and I scheduled an appointment to get a new wig. That might not be so unusual, but this was also the day of her first intravenous dose of BCNU, the chemical that, along with thalidomide, was to be her chemo regime.

Linda seemed to be tolerating the thalidomide treatment very well. Her dosage had been increased to 1000 mg per day – that's twenty huge capsules every night in addition to all her other medications. Dave would break open the bubble-pack packages, put the capsules in a cup, and Linda would bravely swallow them down, a mouthful at a time with the aid of tapioca, ice cream or whatever was available and worked. Dr. Rosenfeld, her neurologist, told us that she must have a cast iron stomach to take all those pills without any nausea, but she did not escape the fatigue that can be associated with this drug.

The two motherly and kind women in the wig shop had known Linda for seven years now. They were experts in working with women – and men – needing hair prostheses, the technical term for a wig. I sensed that they had a special fondness for Linda, partly I'm sure because of her age but also because of the courageous way she coped with the hand she had been dealt.

Linda's previous wig was showing signs of wear. Besides, the steroids she had to take to control swelling on the brain had caused her to gain weight and to have some facial hair that she wanted to cover up. She tried on several wigs until deciding on one that was much longer than the ones she had had before. I wasn't sure that this wig was right for her but she insisted that was the one she wanted. She could still be assertive!

She purchased the wig and we left for St. Luke's. She was quickly settled in one of the recliners for chemo patients and hooked up with the IV of BCNU. I sat in the chair next to her. Before the IV even started, Linda nudged my arm and pointed for me to look. Her left arm, the one with the IV, had started to quiver. Soon she was in a brief but mild seizure. The nurses switched arms and started again. She had two more seizures before the IV was finished four hours later.

The doctor in the office that afternoon did not feel that the IV had caused the seizures and suggested that her dilantin (seizure medicine) level should be checked. He was correct. Her anti-seizure medicine was adjusted and the seizures did not recur. The problem was that even small seizures set back the progress she had made, particularly with speech. The apparent regression in Linda's ability to communicate continued to frustrate all of us.

SOMETIMES VISITORS CAME by late in the afternoon. If they were friends of Linda's and if she seemed to be feeling well, I was able to start for home a little earlier than when I waited for

Dave to come home from work. If Linda had been able to communicate more easily herself, I probably wouldn't have felt the necessity of waiting for someone to be there. But she couldn't. Someone needed to tell Dave about Linda's day, her victories and her setbacks. And so I generally stayed until Dave and Jared got home. After a quick recount of the day for them, and often a stop at the grocery store, I would get on the highway. Even on the days I left early, I usually managed to be in the midst of rush-hour traffic for the thirty-five-mile ride home. The first sixteen of those miles were usually bumper-to-bumper.

As I sat in these traffic jams, the optimism I always had during the day would start to fade. Soon I grabbed my cell phone and began calling anyone who I thought might be home and willing to listen. Frequently I called my brother, Dave. He was always a good listener. Friends Nancy and Jan were regular targets of my phone calls, too. I would also call my parents and my brother, Anthony. By the time I got home, I was feeling either much better or much worse, having vented my frustrations en route.

Lamar would be waiting at home, often with drinks made and sometimes with supper started. He'd gotten some good practice during the nine years I was president of Missouri NEA with my office in Jefferson City. Just as it had been when I was working, the hour or so before dinner was our time to have a cocktail and catch up on each other's day and share stories. This time together was even more important now that I was spending most of my time with Linda while Lamar kept things going at home. But we were dealing with Linda's illness differently. Lamar didn't want to talk much about Linda or what her future might be. It was just too painful. I *had* to talk about Linda because it was so painful. By the time we ate supper at 8:00 or 9:00 in the evening, we were both emotionally exhausted.

May 2001

MAY IS THE traditional month for end-of-school activities and this May was no exception, both for Jared and for Linda.

Jared had two special events at Love and Laughter, his pre-school. The first of these was "Muffins for Mom," held early in the morning on the Friday before Mother's Day, before these working moms had to report to work.

Dave and the school had done everything possible to see that Linda was able to be there for Jared. The little cottage that housed Love and Laughter was built before the days when handicapped accessibility was a requirement. Dave scouted out the route from the car to the school. The front door seemed to offer the best option with fewer stairs and a small, grassy hill. Since Jared's class normally met on the second floor, his teachers had arranged to have his "muffins for mom" set up at a special table on the first floor.

I arrived at Dave and Linda's extra early that morning to help get Jared and Linda ready. It really wasn't necessary. They were ready when I got there. We drove to the school, but just as we pulled into the driveway it started to pour. Undaunted and armed with multiple umbrellas, we managed to get everyone inside without getting too wet in the process.

Dave, as the lone dad in the room, watched from the door as Jared escorted Linda and me to the little table that had been specially set up for us. Jared leaned against Linda's wheelchair, getting as close as he could and proudly introduced his mother to anyone who came into the room. He was beaming, grateful and happy that she was there. She beamed, too, through the tears running down her cheeks.

"Those are happy tears," Jared explained.

LOVE AND LAUGHTER'S end of the year program was Jared's other major event in May. Per instructions, Dave and Jared left the house early. Lamar and I were to follow with Linda, shortly thereafter. Dave and Linda's friend, Laura, were going to make sure that we had seats that would accommodate Linda's chair, too.

Reluctant to get there too early, we lingered more than we should have, miscalculating how long it would take to get Linda to the car and misjudging the length of the drive. By the time we got to the road where the church was located, the clouds had opened up into a spring downpour. It was evident that we were going to be late.

"Turn right," I told Lamar.

Then, noticing street numbers which didn't seem to match, we turned around and went the opposite direction. We kept driving. The street numbers still didn't mesh with what we were looking for, one of the idiosyncrasies of some St. Louis area streets. Perhaps we should have gone the other way after all. We turned around again. Finally, we pulled into the church parking lot ten minutes or so after the program had begun.

Dave and Laura came out to meet us with umbrellas and helped get Linda inside. We had missed the two and three-year-old group, but were just in time for Jared's class. The place that had been saved for Linda was in the middle aisle at the front of the church. I'm sure the parents and grandparents behind us didn't appreciate our coming in late and then blocking their view, but they were gracious just the same.

The four-year-olds sang, Jared waving from his spot in the second row, one of the tallest in the group. His mommy smiled back, beaming as she watched.

We'd made it!

LINDA'S "TEACHER OF the Year" recognition events continued, too. Dave took her to the Parkway Appreciation Dinner while I stayed with Jared. This would give them a night out together and teacher friends would be there to help Linda with the restroom if that were necessary.

It was beginning to take much longer for Linda to do things she had mastered earlier, including applying make-up left-handed. I tried to help but she only got more frustrated. Besides, no matter what she did, it was hard to cover up the blemishes and facial hair caused by the medications. (We later decided that using a depilatory was the only possible solution.)

Finally, she plopped on her new wig, literally. It was not nearly as becoming as her old wig but it gave her some coverage where she felt she needed it most. I think this evening was one of the few times she wore it. Most of the time she preferred just wearing a baseball cap. It was more comfortable and she had enough hair around the fringes that the cap looked quite natural. On other dressier occasions, she reverted to her older wig at Dave's and my urging.

In retrospect, it really didn't matter how the wig looked. She and Dave enjoyed the appreciation dinner and many, many people were glad to see her there.

The following week it was my turn. The Mason Ridge PTO wanted to make sure that she was included in all the special ways that they normally recognized the building's Teacher of the Year. The day of the PTO meeting had been a rough one for Linda, but she gathered her strength, got dressed and we made it to the evening meeting. She was welcomed with hugs from both parents and students. The five fifth graders who had sponsored the Walkathon for Cancer read a special letter in her honor and the PTO added a generous $1000 to their efforts.

The next week, the PTO officers took Linda and me out to lunch. This was another PTO tradition – the teacher part, not the accompanying mom part. Another difference was that Linda had just come from two hours of rehab therapy, instead of simply getting a "lunch out" away from school. It was very special just the same. In a card they presented to Linda they said:

Congratulations, Linda!
We are so proud of your "Teacher of the Year" award! We thank you for your commitment and dedication to the students, families and staff at Mason Ridge.

You have taught our children to read and write. You taught all of us strength, courage, determination and respect! We love you and we thank you for being the incredible person that you are!
The Mason Ridge PTO

MASON RIDGE HAS a long-standing reputation of having an active group of very supportive parents. This was true when I taught in the same building a few years earlier and remains true today. For Linda, the Mason Ridge parents had made her cause, their cause. They'd provided meals in the hospital, shuttled kids to see her and sent many kind notes. They would have done more – anything – but sometimes it was difficult to convey what was needed.

The support of two parents in particular deserve special mention here – Kay and Bridget. Kay, mentioned earlier, was the nurse who had had a young son die of a brain tumor and she had been in the surgery room when Jared was born. Bridget was the mother of Tracey, a very special and very mature fifth grader who had helped organize the walkathon.

Dave had been very reluctant to accept help from outsiders. This was partly due to his strong commitment and sense of responsibility for taking care of his family. He was also uncomfortable accepting help from strangers. It didn't matter that Linda knew them or I knew them – to him, they were still "strangers." Kay and Bridget managed to transcend that perception. They came to the house one day to meet with Dave and me to discuss how they might help.

From that time on, Bridget and Kay were the behind-the-scenes elves who came to help with the cleaning or laundry. They also helped coordinate the delivery of meals to the house. Kay, a master gardener herself, even dug out the overgrown bushes that needed to be replaced and added huge flowerpots in front of the house. Sometimes one of them would just be there to visit with Linda, to keep her company or to take her for a walk around the block. Their presence gave me a chance to finish wallpapering the family room area, a huge task that had been set aside for awhile. The completed project softened the light of the bright-white primer and meant that we could finally remove the wallpapering table, tools and clutter from the room.

Kay and Bridget were wonderful company for me, too.

THE END-OF-SCHOOL year activities were now beginning, giving Linda something to look forward to and helping keep us both centered on what had been our more normal life. I still marvel at the consideration and compassion of Linda's long-term sub, Lisa, who had to compete with this beloved icon.

The most notable of these events was the fifth grade field trip to the St. Louis Zoo in Forest Park. Linda had had many happy hours at the zoo and in Forest Park, as a child, as a mom and as a teacher. With three different fifth grade classes, she had taken advantage of a special educational program the zoo offered, an overnight at the zoo. I joined them as an additional chaperone for these outings. Linda would have the group so well organized and expectations so clearly understood, the overnights were a wonderful learning experience. She made sure that every child got to go. If a child couldn't afford the fee, she arranged for the PTO to sponsor them. I joined the small group of students she always took to dinner before we went to the zoo, kids who didn't have transportation or time to go home before the zoo outing.

At the zoo, the kids learned about animals that were endangered species, saw some of them first-hand and participated in activities that stressed the importance of wildlife preservation. After dark, a zoo guide took the group on a night walk, touring the snake house and observing cheetahs that were actually awake and performing. Fish, small rodents and even a few snakes and spiders stood vigil while we spread our sleeping bags on the floor of the exhibit hall known as "The Living World." Another walk before breakfast yielded bears enjoying a friendly sparring match and keepers and animals beginning their day.

This year's class hadn't been on the overnight, but they had been part of a special preservation project called "Forest Park Forever." With the help of parents providing transportation, they had taken almost monthly trips to Forest Park as part of an environmental study of the balance of nature. Each student had adopted his or her own tree, where they would sit quietly and reflect on what they were seeing around them, recording their thoughts in a special journal. Linda had a special tree, too.

The trips to the park had become a much anticipated and meaningful experience for the kids and they wanted to let Linda know that in some way. Jordyn, one of the girls in Linda's class, suggested that they plant a tree in Forest Park in her honor. With the help of her mother and the cooperation of the sub, the students collected the money and arranged for the tree. They wanted to present their gift to Linda after lunch at the zoo.

We'd had the date for the fifth grade trip to the zoo marked on the calendar for a long time. Jared was invited, too. Although Linda knew about the trip to the zoo, she didn't know about the special honor the kids had planned for her. We arrived at the zoo slightly ahead of the school buses that brought the students and their teachers. Jared was engrossed in the Living World exhibits when we saw the fifth grade come through the entrance. After Jared had satisfied his curiosity with the Living World, I thought we should try to find one of the teachers to find out what the exact plans were for the day. The entire fifth grade class had disappeared, swallowed up in the maze of people and pathways

All right, I thought, we'll start our own tour and surely we'll run into someone we know. I did a quick trip through the Children's Zoo, leaving Jared and Linda at the entrance. No fifth graders there. We wended our way up by the elephants. Still no fifth graders. I soon observed how hilly the zoo really is, something I'd never had to think about when I wasn't pushing a wheelchair. It started to rain – hard. We took shelter along with many other visitors in a small outdoor pavilion.

When it seemed as if the rain would never let up, we moved on. Linda was holding Jared on her lap and he was holding the umbrella. It was a full – and heavy – load. With the umbrella bouncing in front of me I really couldn't see well where we were going. The pavement was slick, now, and we were going downhill. I could envision the wheelchair getting away from me and Linda and Jared going full speed ahead. It didn't happen. We managed to track our way down, going from side to side, switchback fashion, getting only slightly damp in the process but I was certainly relieved when we finally reached the seals and a more level area.

Now the sun chose to reappear and we finally caught the attention of some of our group who knew the schedule.

"OK," said Jared. "Can we go see the snakes, Grandma?"

We started up another hill. Then I looked at my watch and looked at the snake house which still seemed very far away. Finally I told Jared that I thought we'd have to save the snake house for another visit. We turned around and crossed once again to the other side of the zoo. I was really getting my exercise.

Because of the still threatening weather, the kids brought their sack lunches into the ground floor, atrium level of the

Living World building. I left Linda and Jared there – with kids, teachers and parents to keep them company, while I ran back to the car to get our lunches. When I returned, I could look down from the balcony at Linda, surrounded by students giving her hugs and checking out her wheelchair. Jared was being entertained by still other fifth graders. My trek through the zoo in the rain had been well worth it!

After lunch, the kids were loaded into the buses and Jared, Linda and I went to our car. I had been given directions to our next destination. All I'd told Linda was that the kids had something to show her. We were ahead of the buses, but I was watching through my rear view mirror so I wouldn't miss where they turned.

"Keep going," Linda motioned, because she thought we were going to the place where she had taken the kids on many field trips through the Forest Park Forever project.

"I don't think so," I said. "I see the buses turning."

We followed the buses, parked, and with the help of a teacher aide experienced in wheelchair logistics, made our way across the grass to where the young dogwood tree was planted – a very prominent location on St. Louis's Art Hill. Linda was overwhelmed again as the group gathered around her. The sun, by now, prevailed, giving the opportunity for many photos and one-by-one hugs from many of the sixty-or-so fifth graders.

May, 2001

Mason Ridge Student Newsletter, Issue #1

TEACHER OF THE YEAR! Mrs. Linda Favero –
Mrs. Linda Favero was Mason Ridge's Teacher of
the Year and was a finalist for the district Teacher of
the Year.

"She is so nice and encouraging and kind," said
Kristiana. After the first day of school students loved
her and knew what was expected of them and what to
expect from her. Everything was always organized,
except her desk. The students weren't allowed to put
any homework on it because the monster inside the
mess would gobble it up, she would say. Mrs. Favero
expected a lot from her students but they didn't mind.
"She made our subjects interesting and I wasn't bored,"
said Robert. She often told stories about her three year
old son, Jared, and that is what Kristiana will remember
most about her. She expected students to share the
kindness with each other and be polite. All her students
would vote her Teacher of the Year every year if they
could.

Everyone loves and admires her. She makes
learning fun, is always there to talk with and is very
open about her brain tumor. She remains optimistic
about it and everything else. Mason Ridge had several
fundraisers in her honor. The most recent was a
walkathon and many of her past students showed up.
Mrs. Favero has that kind of effect on people.

Anna

Chapter Seven

Keeping Hope Alive

June 5

MAY WHIRLED BY. THERAPY THREE times a week, doctors'
appointments and the whirlwind of end of school-year
activities all helped. By staying busy we managed to shove
thoughts of the upcoming MRI to the back of our minds. Linda
felt – and we all wanted to believe – that the thalidomide and
chemo treatments were working. After all, her speech therapist
had seen some recent improvement and the occupational
therapist had noticed signs of improvement in her ability to
move her right arm and right leg.

Yet, why was she so tired and weak and why was her
speech getting worse? Probably just the chemo, we thought.

Dave had taken Linda to Mason Ridge for "Spirit Day"
and the students versus teachers softball game. I joined her
there and then took her to St. Luke's for the MRI. We would
have two days to wait for the results.

Fortunately, Linda continued to be busy with end of school
events. Dave took her to the fifth grade graduation. Thursday
morning, with the help of Laura and Nancy, she was able to
join the kids for the final day of school at a recreation complex.

That afternoon Dave, Linda and I were all back at Dr.
Cuevas's office in the oncology center for the verdict. We
waited. Finally he came in.

"I'm afraid I have bad news," he reported. "The tumor has
not shrunk. In fact, it has grown another centimeter – from

5 cc to 6 cc." He explained that meant the treatment was not working and there was no point in going forward with the second treatment of BCNU.

"What other options are there?" we asked.

"I think we should try Gleevec," he replied, "but we'll have to see if your insurance will cover it."

Gleevec, or STI 571 as it was known in its clinical trial phase, was thought by some to be the new miracle drug for cancer. It had just been approved by the FDA, but only for leukemia. Clinical trials for the use of Gleevec in the treatment of brain tumors were just beginning. Dr. Cuevas said he would see what he could do.

That evening I stayed at Linda's for dinner and Laura was there, too. We gathered on the patio so Jared could play outside. A hot air balloon appeared overhead, very close to the top of the house. We speculated about what it might be like to be in that balloon and look down on the house and the neighborhood. This speculation led to talk of travel, places we'd been or would like to go.

After Laura left to be with her own family, we stayed on the patio. We were in a state of limbo, not knowing what the next step would be. Dave and I were quiet because we didn't know what to say. Linda was quiet for the same reason and because her speech was so limited now anyway. We were a gloomy looking trio. Slowly Linda looked at Dave and then at me and then she got a small smile on her face, raising her left eyebrow in a way she had when thinking of something.

"What is it?" Dave asked.

She shook her head, obviously thinking of something but unable to respond. We knew it was something pleasant or amusing for she kept smiling.

"Do you want us to guess what it is?"

Linda nodded. So we began the game of twenty questions again, something we'd utilized often these past few months. We started the discovery process. We determined that it was something she wanted and that something would cost over $1000. Her chuckle and positive response to the question of cost had relaxed the atmosphere. I thought of the hot air balloon and the talk about travel.

"Do you want to go on a trip?" I asked. Again a positive nod.

"Where would you like to go?"

Linda shrugged her shoulders. We started naming places and found it really didn't matter. She just wanted to go on a trip to someplace she had never been before.

Dave agreed that a trip might be just what they both needed.

June 8

I HADN'T SLEPT much that night. Between exploring trip possibilities and researching Gleevec and clinical trials, I was on the computer most of the night.

I arrived early the next morning to find that Linda and Dave had not had a good night either. She'd been restless and nauseous. Dave had given her some pain medication and she was finally sleeping.

Dave left for work and I started making phone calls to Wisconsin and Texas where clinical trials were being conducted for Gleevec. Again, the answer was that although she seemed to fit the profile, she needed to be independently mobile which she was not. I asked one of the people I spoke with a question that had been on my mind, "Even if we can 'cure' the tumor, can we cure the brain damage?"

Although they couldn't say anything for sure without knowing more about Linda's case, they said that the answer to that question was probably, "No."

Laura arrived shortly before noon, dressed in a pretty long, pale pink dress, ready for the special outing we had planned for the day – high tea at the Ritz. I had treated Linda and Laura to high tea at the Ritz once before, when Linda was the bride-to-be and Laura was her maid of honor so very long ago. We had planned this occasion to celebrate the end of school and the hoped-for good news from this MRI.

When Laura and I went to Linda's room where she had been sleeping, it was obvious that we would not be going to high tea or anywhere else that day. I kept going back to the bedroom to check on Linda. Throughout this ordeal she had been fortunate never to have had too much pain or nausea. Today was certainly the exception. Even morphine, which we'd used at home only one other time, didn't seem to help much.

Laura helped me get Linda to the bathroom, wash her face and then help her back to bed. With Linda settled and resting again, Laura hiked up her long skirt and got up on the bed to sit crossed-legged next to Linda, holding her hand.

"Don't worry!" she said. "We'll go another time, when you're feeling better."

I left the room but Laura stayed with Linda all that afternoon. Finally, she laid down next to Linda and they talked and laughed and cried, sharing memories, sharing hopes and sharing fears but most of all, sharing friendship and love. It was exactly what Linda needed and much more important than any high tea anywhere.

Nancy came, ready for high tea too, but stayed to help. Kay and Bridget and Jan and Connie and Debbie and Karen also came, helping out at various times during that day.

Dave called that afternoon. Dr. Cuevas had called him and said the insurance company's response for Gleevec had been negative. He had also tried to see if he could obtain Gleevec directly from the manufacturer, Norvatis, but the response there was the same. Dr. Cuevas recommended that it was time we call in hospice. Dave asked what I thought and I reluctantly agreed.

A nurse from hospice arrived that evening about suppertime. She would not be the regular nurse that would be with us but would get the paperwork started. The process seemed to take an incredibly long time. Jan helped by keeping Jared occupied outside. He was playing with his trucks in the mulch, a child's simple pleasure, oblivious to the serious nature of the discussion inside.

The nurse explained the purpose of hospice to us. Hospice care requires that no aggressive treatment is being done, just medications to make the patient comfortable and improve the quality of her life. We were assured that if we did find a clinical trial for which Linda was eligible, we could opt out of hospice.

I asked about therapy. "Could that continue?"

The nurse wasn't sure but would check. Perhaps because of Linda's young age, the insurance company would allow it. I just hated to see Linda regress anymore if we could find a treatment that worked.

Support services would begin at once, so we had someone to call if we had problems over the weekend. The nurse left, but not before Linda got violently ill, vomiting horrible green bile. She was weak and tired and hurting. Calling in hospice had been the right decision.

Linda Update, June 9

TODAY MARKS THE starting point of the rest of this journey. Dave's mom is coming from Illinois to stay with them. We will all be grateful for her extra hand and support. I'm sure many of you will be pitching in to help or dropping by to visit, too. Please understand, however, that if you ask what we need help with or when is a "good" time we may not be able to tell you. We are taking one day, one hour at a time.

Throughout these updates I have tried to be positive. These notes have been my therapy and your responses have been my emotional support. I must end this update on a positive note.

Seven years ago when Linda was first diagnosed, she was told to forget about ever having children. Surgery was not an option because of the location of the tumors so she had radiation therapy. That worked and we have our "miracle baby." When Jared was almost two, new growth appeared. Linda was part of a phase III clinical trial for Temodar and that worked, too. At least until last year.

Throughout this time Linda has been able to enjoy family, friends and teaching. Receiving the Mason Ridge Teacher of the Year award – and the response from all her students and parents – past and present has been incredible and helped her get through this. As she said to me once in the hospital, "I didn't realize how much difference I was making." I replied, "Most of us never have that opportunity."

We have brought home from school her personal things and books – and more books. We brought home the giant, three-foot pencil presented to her and her class for their participation in the D.A.R.E. program. We brought home the beautiful chair that a mom and her students presented to her two years ago. Next week we will pick up the director's chair presented to Linda by this year's students, designed by Taryn.

School is over. Linda's classroom is bare. But we will continue to do everything possible to help her enjoy this summer.

Keep praying for a miracle! Thanks for all your help and support.

Martha

AND A RESPONSE from a Mason Ridge parent:

June 9

Dear Mrs. Karlovetz:

It is hard to know what to say. I hope my words will help more than hurt. You, Linda, Dave and Jared are often in my thoughts.

A few weeks ago my third grade Sunday school class studied the parable of the Prodigal Son. There were two lessons to learn from the story. The first I told them was that of forgiveness, which the adventuring son receives when his reckless lifestyle leaves him in a field sharing slop fed to pigs. We felt pretty good about both giving and receiving forgiveness.

The second half of the story was harder to grasp. The obedient son, who had behaved well and done everything his father had ever asked, was a little annoyed when this errant brother returned and was greeted with such celebration. His father comforted him, saying, "Everything I own is yours, but we must celebrate because your brother who was lost has come back."

I asked my students to think about their own brothers and sisters and how each needed different things at different times, but how their parents took care of each of them, just like the father in the story. After a long moment of silence one boy looked up from the table to blurt out, "It isn't fair!"

And he was right. It wasn't fair, and we want it to be. Just like that older brother we want our fair share of all that life offers. We want it for us, and for our children, and for our friends. But that doesn't happen. Even good and obedient sons know pain and a sense of loss.

God doesn't offer us fair. What he does offer is the forgiveness the younger brother in this story received; compassion such as that shown by God to his people in the desert over and over again, and his abiding presence in our lives. Often that takes the form of a caring parent. You are without a doubt that presence in Linda's life, Mrs. Karlovetz.

Like my little third grade student, a part of me says about this illness, it isn't fair. But you already knew that. I will keep praying for a miracle for Linda. I also rejoice that she is able to know the compassion and presence of so many loving family members and friends.

Thank you for keeping us posted on Linda. I enjoyed a minute with her at the fifth grade play day on Thursday. She is as lovely as ever.

Dawn

KAREN, DAVE'S FRIEND from work, stayed that night to help with Jared and Linda. Rachel arrived on Saturday. Linda seemed to be feeling a little better and there were plenty of hands to help out so I went home. I returned Sunday, unable to stay away.

When I arrived Sunday morning, Linda was sitting up in her wheelchair at the kitchen table, eating and able to smile and give me a hug. She even seemed to be getting some speech back. Rachel reported that Linda no longer needed the morphine, which meant she was more awake and more alert.

Perhaps it was just the effects of the thalidomide wearing off, but thinking of the hospice visit, I thought, "Did we give up too soon?"

On Monday morning I was back on the phone trying to find a way to get Gleevec. I discovered that individuals may buy the drug if you are able to get a doctor's prescription, but it's very expensive. I was beginning to fully understand what it means when you hear that it's the insurance companies making the life and death decisions.

I called the insurance company. I wanted to see if therapy could be continued even if Linda was in hospice. I also wanted to see if they would reconsider the decision about Gleevec. Here I ran into another obstacle. Because I was not Linda's legal guardian, Dave would have to give the insurance company authorization to talk with me. While he readily did that and although I certainly understood the reason for the policy, under the circumstances it was hard to swallow. When I did finally get through to them, I had to repeat the story to what seemed like an endless number of people. At one point I was told that her case file had been closed since she was now in hospice care.

"Look," I said. "She's only thirty-two-years old and deserves to have every possible medical treatment available. The reason she's in hospice is because we can't get the insurance company to approve Gleevec. By the time Gleevec has been through the clinical trials for brain tumors it will be too late for her."

Finally the insurance company agreed to review the case.

That afternoon, the hospice nurse who would be the regular nurse for Linda made her first home visit. Dave had called her more than once during the night on Friday and she had been very helpful. The nurse explained in more detail the services hospice could provide. We declined home health care because Linda didn't need it. The nurse then took Linda's vital signs – blood pressure, pulse and temperature, something she said would be done on every visit. As I expected, Linda's vital signs were normal as they had been throughout most of her illness. The nurse visited for awhile and then left.

I felt uneasy but didn't say anything. The entire time the nurse had been there she didn't even seem to try to interact with Linda. Although Linda was sitting in her wheelchair right next to her – fully comprehending everything even if she couldn't talk, the nurse seemed to direct her remarks to everyone but her. Perhaps it was Linda's youth that bothered her or perhaps she didn't really believe Linda could understand. I decided to withhold judgement for now.

When the nurse returned two days later, her manner was the same. In fact, she'd even forgotten her stethoscope so she couldn't check Linda's vital signs. Rachel was with us now and her reaction – and Linda's – were much the same. After she left, we decided to request a different nurse from hospice.

Debbie the nurse (as we called her to differentiate between Linda's teaching partner, Debbie) was her replacement. She was wonderful – very compassionate with Linda and very sympathetic to my cause of trying to find a source for Gleevec and trying to maintain the therapy. She understood.

Sandy the social worker also paid a visit. She was tall and thin and about Linda's age. She was very direct and frank in her remarks but seemed to connect with Linda right away. When I mentioned that we were still trying to pursue treatment, she brought up the issue of quality of life. Looking directly at Linda, she asked, "Do you feel you currently have quality of life?"

Without hesitation, Linda nodded and replied, "Yes!"

I'm sure her answer surprised this professional young social worker. Viewed from Linda's perspective, she did have quality of life. She certainly had hundreds of people who knew about her and cared for her. She was still able to enjoy the sun and the birds, Jared and Dave, and eating a good meal. She still wanted to go on a trip to some place that neither she nor Dave had been to before. Admittedly, this was not the quality of life she had known before, but it was still quality of life.

Pastor Paul, from hospice, and Pastor Amy, from Manchester Methodist, also came by. Pastor Paul met mostly with Rachel and me for Linda was sleeping. He remarked on the posters and mementos that had been brought home from school and remembered seeing the television coverage of the walkathon.

Linda was awake when Amy came and she was able to visit with her privately. I was sure that Linda had questions to ask and fears and hopes to express – difficult to do when you can't talk. Amy suggested that we sit with her, sharing pictures and just talking. We promised to do that.

FREQUENTLY ON MY thirty-five-mile drive home in traffic, I would call friends and family to update them. One of these calls was usually to my mother who was safely back in her assisted living residence outside Syracuse. She was not doing well herself. Eighty-nine years of living and fifty years of smoking were catching up with her. Almost every time I called to give her the latest report, she would ask, "But what about her hands?"

"Her hands are the least of our worries," I would reply, as patiently as possible. "I used to think paralysis was bad. It is. But the loss of the ability to communicate – to talk, to read and to write – and yet still know everything you want to say, is far worse."

Speech was returning again so perhaps the loss of speech wasn't permanent but simply the result of fatigue and the effects of the chemo.

These calls were a way to keep my mother informed. They also gave me a chance to catch up on how she was doing. Often she would say, "It's not fair! It's my turn!" Sometimes she would say, "It's time."

I remember telling her, "You've just got to hang in there now. I can't handle both of you at once!"

HOSPICE CARE CONTINUED for that week and on into the next. It was minimal because we really didn't need much more at the time. Linda was feeling so much better. One of the first things they suggested, we implemented immediately – keeping a logbook of Linda's medications and condition. With so many people coming in and out, the log made the complicated regime much easier to track.

Linda continued to improve. We used Tylenol and a patch for pain and headaches. These were much easier on her system than morphine. On Monday, Linda resumed outpatient therapy with the insurance company's nod of approval. On her first day back she had an excellent session with Laura, the occupational therapist, did well with Lynn in speech but was too tired to continue with Trish for physical therapy.

Trish and Barb, her former occupational therapist, had volunteered to come to the house occasionally after work. They thought they might be able to help with accessibility questions in the new house and do some therapy as well. Most importantly, the help they offered was moral support, for they had become good friends with Linda.

With their help, Linda (and Dave and I) had a major victory on Trish and Barb's first visit. For two months we had talked about trying to get Linda downstairs to see the fully finished lower level of her new home. Every newcomer to visit had gotten a tour of the house – including the basement – but Linda had never seen it. We had never had the right combination of time, helpers and energy to accomplish this.

Now, with Trish's expertise and three of us to help, we maneuvered our way down the stairs. It was a slow process, for Linda's right leg was incredibly weak and she had lost much of her sense of balance. I'm sure Trish questioned her wisdom in even making the offer to help her downstairs. But taking one step at a time, we made it. She was exhausted and crying by the time we finished the trip but some of those were happy tears.

Almost two months after they had moved in, Linda finally got to see the rest of her new home!

I CONTINUED MY pursuit of finding an affordable source for Gleevec. I checked again for clinical trials and even requested copies of her medical records and most recent MRIs just in case I found one that would be a possibility for Linda. I asked the triage nurse at the oncologist's office if she thought I was crazy to do this. She reassured me that she would be doing the same thing if Linda were her daughter.

People suggested I check the Internet, but Dr. Cuevas warned us to check these sources very carefully before buying. I discovered that Gleevec was not yet available in either Canada or the United Kingdom because it hadn't been approved by their equivalent of our FDA. We could order it through an Internet pharmacy at $2258 for a month's supply, but we could also get it right at St. Luke's pharmacy – a pharmacy we knew and trusted – for $2500.

I called Dr. Butler, the radiation oncologist who had followed Linda's case for years, and asked him to review Linda's latest MRIs. With Dr. Butler, we had grown accustomed to seeing the MRIs and even imagining that we could interpret them a little. Dr. Cuevas, however, relied on the radiologist's report which was much more accurate but left us without the benefit of the startling visual perspective of the scans.

Dr. Butler reviewed the latest results and then called me. He reported that the overall tumor mass was now about 9 x 6 x 4 centimeters. He said that even though that wasn't what we had hoped, considering the total mass of her (three) tumors, the growth in the last two months had been slow. It was the small tumor in the rear that was most worrisome now, having grown from one to five centimeters since December.

"What's the tumor officially called?" I asked, needing this information to be accurate as I contacted various clinical trials.

"It's labeled as a Grade IV oliogoglioblastoma with multiforme characteristics."

From what I knew about the world of brain tumor research, "glioblastoma" and "multiforme" are very frightening terms, words no one wants to hear.

Knowing Linda's determination and spirit, and perhaps knowing Dave and Jared and me, Dr. Butler did think we should continue to investigate getting Gleevec.

I shared this information with Dave. The issues about continuing treatment – and there were many – would impact him much more than they did me. He was the one who would have to get up several times during the night when Linda needed help going to the bathroom. He was the one who would be living with the side affects of the medication. He was the one who would be paying for the Gleevec if it weren't covered by insurance. He was also the one who would be impacted for a lifetime if Gleevec did prove to be the "miracle" drug we were looking for. The odds against Linda ever being able to return to teaching or to "normal" were increasing every day.

In addition to my notations in the log that day, I left Dave a note:

*Dav*e:

Regarding Gleevec: From what I've been reading on the Internet, I (too) have many questions about the side effects of this drug. I also noted that some doctors are suggesting that Gleevec be taken in combination with Temodar – the chemo Linda had three years ago with few side effects. These are questions we can ask Dr. Cuevas when we meet with him on Thursday.

The decision as to whether or not to pursue another form of treatment is ultimately Linda's. If insurance covers it and it's the right treatment, that's great. If it's too new and untried (for brain tumors) but is still the right treatment, that decision should be made independently of the financial question. Would she take Gleevec if insurance did cover the prescription? Many people would be more than willing to help, some directly and some through fundraisers. As with other chemo treaments you would probably know in two or three months if this one were working.

Martha

THE NEXT DAY Linda, Dave and I met with Dr. Rosenfeld, her very compassionate neurologist. Yes, he concurred, the tumor had grown. Yes, the growth was significant. No, the tumor in the part of the brain that controls verbal functions was not growing (more) at this time. However, pressure from the tumor swelling could be affecting her ability to speak, her moods and her decision-making processes. Yes, he agreed, Linda should go ahead with this new treatment if Dr. Cuevas felt it offered hope.

June 21

DR. CUEVAS HAD been on vacation for a week, saving him a lot of phone calls from us. We scheduled an appointment with him to talk more about treatment options even if the insurance company wouldn't cover them. Dave, Lamar, Linda and I all waited again in yet another consultation room for a doctor to meet with us.

"What about using Temodar again?" I asked, based on the information I had gotten from the Internet. "It worked once, couldn't it possibly work again?"

Patiently, and probably thinking that a little medical knowledge can be dangerous in the hands of lay people, Dr. Cuevas explained that since her tumor had ultimately reoccurred, Temodar had not been successful, medically speaking. With that question out of the way, the discussion turned to Gleevec.

Dr. Cuevas was very honest and straightforward with us. We felt fortunate that he was young and progressive. We also felt fortunate that he had some experience with Gleevec when it was in the clinical trial stage for leukemia.

He explained that the side effects were what every chemo can cause – liver toxicity, low blood count, some swelling.

"Will it work?" we asked.

"I just can't tell you that," he replied. "It has worked on rats. It has had a forty to fifty percent success rate with CM Leukemia. I can't even tell you what the right dosage is for glioblastomas; no one knows. We'll start with 400 mg (four tablets per day), the recommended dosage for leukemia."

Dr. Cuevas added that he would be monitoring Linda's case very closely. If the treatment succeeded, the results would be publishable. We would also lose hospice care because a patient in hospice care can't be receiving treatment at the same time.

"How long will it take before we know anything?"

"About six weeks."

And then I asked the question that had been nagging at me for quite some time. "Would you prescribe this if Linda were your wife or daughter?"

Slowly and thoughtfully, Dr. Cuevas responded. "That's a good question."

Then, looking directly at Linda he said, "I try to treat all my patients as if they are my family. Yes, I would prescribe this even if you were my wife or daughter."

With Linda nodding in agreement, Dave said, "Write the prescription."

The triage nurse came in for the blood tests. We were breaking new ground in medical history. What we really needed was a miracle!

DAVE RETURNED TO work and Lamar went home. I took Linda to therapy and, while she was there, took the prescription that I had fought so hard to obtain to the hospital pharmacy. I was on a first name basis with the pharmacists by now. I asked them to try putting the prescription through the insurance, but that if it was turned down, we were prepared to pay for it. They said that they would have to order it anyway so it would be at least the following Monday before they would have the Gleevec in stock.

After lunch and another therapy session, Linda and I were getting ready to leave the hospital when my cell phone rang. It was the pharmacy. Some of my earlier, badgering phone calls had paid off.

"Martha, we have good news for you. The insurance company will cover the prescription for Gleevec."

Linda was looking at me inquisitively. I dialed Dave's number at work and shared the news with both of them simultaneously. Then, right there in the hospital vestibule, Linda and I hugged and shared tears of relief.

With the question of treatment resolved for the moment, I returned to planning the trip that Linda wanted to take. Since retirement I had been working as a part-time travel agent, and trip planning was something I did with a relish. A cruise sounded like an initial possibility because once they were on board ship, they wouldn't have to worry about luggage and getting around. They'd also been on a cruise. One of Dave's relatives had graciously treated them to a cruise when Linda finished her radiation treatments and appeared to be well on the road to recovery. Besides, a cruise posed the question of what might happen if Linda got ill and had to return. No, a cruise was not going to be possible.

They finally settled on a trip to the Oregon shore. They could fly non-stop from St. Louis and rent a car. I found a resort on the coast that had handicapped-equipped rooms. Reservations were made. Airline tickets were purchased.

The date was set. Linda and Dave were to leave St. Louis on August 19. The flight departed at 11:05 a.m.

BECAUSE LINDA WAS feeling so much better, she and Jared came to our house for the weekend, giving Dave a break and Linda and Jared a change of scenery.

Laura brought them out along with her son, Todd, who was just a year older than Jared. Laura took the two boys down to the lake to supervise a swim. Then Lamar asked Linda if she'd like to try to go down to the lake on the ATV. She thought for a moment and nodded that she'd like to give it a try. With some careful maneuvering, Lamar and I managed to get her from the wheelchair to the back of the ATV. Linda held onto her daddy with her good arm and off they went, down the 150 foot path to the lake. I had to close my eyes – I couldn't watch. But they did make it safely to the park-like area we have next to the lake. Linda was thus able to spend an hour or so watching Jared and Todd splash in the water together.

Laura went home before dinner but Linda and Jared stayed. That evening we savored all the little things that people do, a quiet family dinner, a bubble bath for Jared in the jacuzzi and several bedtime stories. The next morning for breakfast we had scrambled eggs and one of Linda's favorites, home fried potatoes.

These so simple, everyday things are much more meaningful when you aren't sure how long they will be possible.

SINCE APRIL I had been scheduled to go to the NEA Convention in Los Angeles. Had Linda still been with hospice, I wouldn't even have considered going. I had thought about canceling anyway but Linda insisted that I go. She was feeling better and Rachel would be there to help out during the day and to take Linda to therapy. I packed my bags and made everyone promise that I would be called home immediately if things changed for the worse.

Linda Update, July 3

THIS IS AN update from afar – Los Angeles, California, to be exact, the site of the NEA Convention. Although some of you that receive this update are here, many of you are not. Yes, I'm here at my first convention in six years but it does get in your blood. Besides, thanks to cell phones and computers, I can stay in touch and leave in a moment's notice if I have to – but I haven't.

I was going to write an update last Tuesday night before I left but just didn't have time. Here it is, a week late just because Tuesday was really special, special because Linda was communicating more than she has been able to do recently. I first noticed it when I arrived. She was up and dressed, looking very pleased with herself. She had finally achieved getting dressed one handed – try it sometime, especially fastening a bra.

Through that unique way she now has of communicating, part verbal, part gesturing, and part shaking her head "yes" or "no," she was able to let me know that she wanted to drive by the tree her kids had planted for her in Forest Park. Dave's mom, sister and two kids were coming that night and on Thursday there were plans for the zoo. Linda wanted to make sure she could find the tree. So on the way back from doing some errands we made a big loop through Forest Park. She kept pointing and giving directions. But what she had in mind was not the tree the kids had planted, but a tree and a pond where she had taken her class as part of their Forest Park Forever project. It seemed out of the way to me but she knew exactly where she was going and why. Park construction blocked our way and we had to settle for looking for the tree that had been planted. That tree we found easily and got out to admire it. I wish I had had a camera!

On our way home from the beauty parlor that afternoon she let me know she had two things she wanted to do. The first was to get ice cream. That was easy and she was even able to say the words. The second was more difficult. Again, she directed me by motioning and pointing until I got the message – she wanted to go pick up Jared at pre-school, which we did. How much we take the gift of speech for granted!

Tuesday was such a good day I even teased her about "faking it" just so I wouldn't cancel my trip. Brain tumor headaches, however, are something no one could fake – or ignore. But she hasn't had any recently. She has had some days when she has been completely exhausted. These also make her very emotional partially because of where the tumor is causing pressure on the right side of her brain (the tumor is actually on the left.) She has also been having many good days and has seemed pleased and happy when I've called her from here. Yesterday, Rachel, Dave's mom, reported that Linda had put on make-up for the first time in weeks. She had done well in therapy, too. In occupational therapy, they cheered when she was able to raise her right arm by herself. She also was able to move her fingers for the first time since January.

Now, before anyone gets their hopes up too much, I have to say that this is probably not because of the new, experimental chemo, Gleevec. More likely it is the result of the thalidomide wearing off. Whatever is causing it, we'll take the positive results!

For the Fourth of July, Linda, David, Jared and Rachel are joining Lamar and the Bierks at the lake. On the fifth she has an appointment with her chemo doctor. Lamar's going too so I can get the inside report I'm so used to getting when I'm there. There probably won't be too much to report. Dr. Cuevas told us that it will be at least six weeks before we'll know if the Gleevec is working.

Each student "adopted" their special tree in Forest Park.

One student wrote, "We felt at peace here."

Even the teacher adopted a tree.

So, two weeks down, four to go, but who's counting! Keep those prayers coming!"

Martha

LINDA CONTINUED TO do well while I was in Los Angeles, making
it much easier for me to enjoy the convention. When I called
home on the Fourth of July, Lamar reported that he and Dave
had managed to get Linda on the ATV, down our hill, out onto
our boat dock and then onto the boat! Linda cried when the
mission was accomplished – so pleased was she to be doing
something that seemed so impossible. Nancy recounted Linda's
joy in seeing one of the beautiful blue herons that live on the
lake. "Ahhhh!" she smiled as she pointed out the heron.

Linda was doing so well I even told her in one call home
that perhaps I should go out of town more often. It was easy to
be lulled into a sense of complacency.

Weekend of July 13-15

PRIOR TO MY leaving the convention, my brothers had made
arrangements to come for a visit. Although Nancy, Anthony's
wife, had a previous family commitment and could not come,
Tina, Dave's wife, would be here. Tina, a cancer survivor
herself, had always been an inspiration to Linda. The time also
coincided with my birthday.

Before we left for our house at the lake, Linda and I stopped
at the grocery store. I had just the normal grocery shopping
before a weekend to do, but Linda had two items she was intent
on purchasing. First she insisted on buying some cookies, even
though we planned to make some. These were not just any
cookies she wanted to buy but Vienna Fingers. I thought she
just wanted them for her home but she made sure the package
was in the sacks destined to come to the lake. She remembered
that Vienna Fingers were a favorite of my brother Dave's.

For her second purchase, Linda motioned for me to start
checking out while she wheeled her grocery-cart wheelchair
to a nearby rack of greeting cards. The next day she presented
me with the card, almost apologetically for she often had done
so much more for my birthday. Although she had painstakingly

signed the card inside, on the outside of the bright yellow envelope she had also written – Linda.

I hugged her and thanked her and put the card on display. Later, I threw it away, reluctant to keep any reminders of just how much brain damage there had already been. Nevertheless, I will never forget that card.

We spent Saturday enjoying family and lake. Tina remarked that although Linda's speech had suffered, she still attempted to discipline Jared, his name being one of the few words she could say spontaneously with any consistency. "Jared!" she would say, in a tone that implied obedience and attention. She also maintained her sense of humor, commenting "silly" at one of Jared's antics.

We had a wonderful afternoon by the water. Lamar took Linda down the hill on the ATV, whistling all the way. With the help of my brothers, Lamar even got Linda down to the dock again, this time to get her feet in the water. She wanted to go swimming but none of us was sure that we would be able get her out of the water once we had succeeded in getting her in. So she had to be content with dangling her feet off the edge of the dock.

Dave joined us for dinner that evening and spent the night. The next morning, however, he was unusually tense. He sat at the dining room table doing some paperwork, politely refusing any of the company-style continental breakfast I had prepared.

Lamar had taken Anthony to the airport, Linda and Jared were still sleeping and my brother, Dave, was out for a run. Dave's silence continued, making me increasingly nervous. I had so hoped for a happy morning and breakfast. The silence continued even after Tina joined us. By the time my brother had returned from his run, I was ready for a very uncharacteristic (for me) walk. Dave and Tina joined me, reassuring and comforting me along the way.

Whatever was bothering Dave that morning – and he had plenty of things to be stressed about – had dissipated by dinner that night when we all went out for dinner at a local steak place. Perhaps in his silence, he was remembering the same weekend just one year before. Linda had planned and executed a very special surprise party for my sixtieth – something she couldn't possibly have accomplished now.

July 16

MY NEPHEW, JON, called. He and his wife, Shirra, were the proud new parents of Karis, a beautiful little girl born this day – my birthday.

"Congratulations!" I said.

"What a beautiful gift you have. Treasure her always," I thought.

Karis's birth gave Linda and me an excuse to go to the mall to shop and have lunch after therapy. As we had so many times in the past, we oohed and aahed over baby clothes and spent more money than we should have to welcome this new addition to the family.

Life goes on. But this was our last shopping expedition.

THERAPY CONTINUED AND Linda seemed to be doing OK. At least, that's what I rationalized. She was, after all on some very potent medications. In a routine visit with her oncologist, the decision was made to continue with Gleevec for another five weeks. The next MRI would be scheduled in late August.

Linda and Jared came out to the lake for part of the weekend. She slept much of the time so we didn't get a chance to go down to the lake again. We did make a short trip, but not to the lake. A stray kitten had wandered its way into our yard. I had called a local animal sanctuary. They thought they could find a good home for the stray. Linda decided she would like to join me on this mission so we loaded Jared, the kitten, the wheelchair and ourselves into the van. The drive between our home and Union, Missouri, twenty miles away, passes through Ozark foothills, scenic wine country and the Missouri River bottomlands. The weather was reasonably cool on this beautiful July day. The "Raffi" tape was playing to keep Jared entertained. Linda, sitting next to me, was nodding her head back and forth in rhythm with the music, smiling broadly.

"You're enjoying this ride, aren't you?" I asked. She nodded affirmatively. The beautiful scenery was a change of pace from the trips of necessity we had been making almost every day.

Life seemed beautiful in spite of the struggles.

DURING THE NEXT week, Linda seemed to regress even more. She fell one morning trying to reach something on a closet shelf, pulling the loaded closet rod with her. Lifeline came to the rescue, calling Dave at work. By the time I got there, Dave had returned to work and Linda was laughing about her fall. "Help! Help! I've fallen and can't get up," she quipped, mimicking the Lifeline ad.

Linda was more emotional than usual and she had difficulty even transferring out of her wheelchair. In physical therapy, Trish noticed that she appeared to have lost peripheral vision on her right side. She needed that peripheral vision to give her legs the clues they needed to function. I had also learned that the steroid she had been on since January, Decadron, could have some significant side effects including the loss of vision. Of course, her tumor could have been causing this, too!

I shared this information with the oncologist triage nurse. She called the neurologist who was on call while Dr. Rosenfeld was out of town. She promptly requested an MRI for the next day, followed by an appointment in her office. In some respects this was a relief. Rather than waiting until the end of August, we would know now if the Gleevec was having the desired effect. We would also know whether medications or tumor were causing some of the noticeable side effects she was exhibiting.

As I reported in the *Update* that evening:

Linda Update, July 23

THE BEST CASE scenario for tomorrow: the tumor is stable, medications are causing the problem. Linda may have to alter, reduce or "take a holiday" from some.

Worst case scenario: the symptoms are from the tumor growing; discontinue treatment.

I continue to be a pragmatic optimist. Linda has not had a seizure in several weeks. She has only had to take pain medication for "tumor" headaches, the really severe kind, a couple of times since early June. I therefore believe that the medication causality is certainly possible. That gets my vote and I know it gets all of yours.

Please indulge in a little extra prayer tomorrow. We'll let you know how things turn out.

Martha

Linda Update, July 24

LAST NIGHT I outlined two scenarios. I didn't expect that both would be true. Yes, Linda is experiencing some side effects from the steroids but "long term" means years, not months, and their usage is necessary to keep the swelling down on the brain. In fact, the neurologist even increased the dosage slightly.

But yes, too, the tumor has grown since June 5, Linda's last MRI. The neurologist and the neurosurgeon both reviewed the MRI scans to see if additional surgery was a possible option. It is not. The tumor is too large and too deep into the brain. The chemo-oncologist will not review the MRI report until tomorrow.

At this point, Linda will probably continue on Gleevec for another five weeks, take the MRI that was already scheduled and we'll see where we are then. There really are no other alternatives.

So, we continue to take one day at a time and will try to make each of Linda's days the best they can possibly be.

Martha

ON THE WAY home from the appointment with the neurologist, Linda and I stopped at Mason Ridge. The principal had called to say that there were still some personal things in Linda's room even though Dave had brought home several boxes at the end of the school year. We stopped to see if anything that remained would be something she would want to keep.

I had heard the rumor that Linda's classroom was going to be changed for the following year but hadn't had the courage to tell her. Although her medical leave would continue, the school had to make plans for the upcoming school year. Linda's classroom had been slated to receive special computer equipment for satellite learning. Since in all probability she wouldn't be there to start the year, the plan was to move her classroom across the hall. I was unaware that the move had already been made.

The building was quiet and dark when we got there, a shadow of what it would be in just a few weeks. Linda's room was open but starkly empty. The room across the hall where her things had been taken was locked. I left Linda sitting in the hall and found a custodian who unlocked the room and let us in. Stacked in boxes, along a cabinet at the back of the room, were the years of teaching materials and books she had accumulated. The kids had helped pack them and carefully labeled them. I explained what I knew of the move to Linda as we looked through some of her things.

She sorted out an old sweater she was fond of to give to Debbie and a couple of books and photo albums she kept as a record of each year's class. The rest, she decided, should stay. I knew she was upset by what she had seen. As we headed out of the building, we had to retrace our steps past the classroom where she – and so many kids – had spent some wonderful years. The only evidence remaining to identify the room as hers was hanging from the doorknob – a marker with a picture of Garfield the cat and the words, "Linda's Room." She reached for it, defiantly, and yanked it from the doorknob.

We were both silent as we left the building.

Dr. Cuevas was supposed to review the MRI on Thursday. He may have done so but he didn't call us to report. We didn't call him either, or even mention it among ourselves. We were too afraid of what we might hear.

On Friday, Linda went to therapy. She dressed up, wearing a dress and her wig rather than her usual ball cap because we were finally going to take our trip to the Ritz for high tea that afternoon. Laura continued to note progress with the use of her arm but speech therapy was a different story. She had difficulty even identifying common objects, something she had re-mastered just a few months ago. Lynn theorized that this difficulty might have been caused by the emotional stress of the latest MRI. Linda nodded in the affirmative and I readily agreed.

Nancy and friend Laura joined us at the hospital and we left for the Ritz. Except for the wheelchair, our foursome looked like any foursome of women who might be celebrating a special occasion at the Ritz. We were almost too eager, arriving promptly at 2:00 p.m., the first customers to be seated. We were relieved when other customers finally arrived and were seated at nearby tables. Somehow, it made the outing more festive. When a very dainty first course of miniature appetizers were served, we joked that we hoped there was more, but not so the waiter could hear us. Soon other courses arrived.

We talked and reminisced and talked some more, none of us really addressing the issue that was our greatest concern. Linda spilled a small tidbit on the front of her dress. A few minutes later, Nancy had a similar accident. Linda laughed that now someone else had a spot on the front of her dress – and she had two good hands. We laughed and talked and laughed some more. All casual small talk. Continuing in that vein, Laura innocently asked, "Mrs. Karlovetz, where are you planning to go on your next trip?"

"We don't have anything planned right now," I replied and looked at Linda. Silent tears were coming down her cheeks. I reached over and grabbed her hand.

"Don't worry!" I said. "We'll have plenty of time for trips when we get this behind us. Right now there isn't a place I'd rather be."

None of us knew that this would be our last excursion.

Chapter Eight

The Classroom is Bare

THE WEEKEND WAS PEACEFUL. DAVE, Jared and Linda spent it together. On Sunday afternoon they took Jared to another child's birthday party at Chuck E Cheese. The rest of the time they spent as a family.

I stayed home, restless and worried most of the time, but not wanting to interfere. On Monday I drove into town, not arriving at Linda's until about 9:45 a.m. – in time to take her to therapy. We had still been trying to give her some time alone. I thought I would find her in the family room, ready and dressed as she had been recently. Instead, she was nowhere to be seen. I raced back to the bedroom and found her sitting in her wheelchair in front of the bathroom door. She was looking at the toilet but didn't seem to know what to do or was unable to find the strength to do it. I helped her to the toilet and then back to bed. She was obviously too exhausted to go to therapy and slept most of the day.

I called Dave at work and he said she'd had a restless night. He mentioned that he was getting concerned about the trip. He wondered if Linda would be up to it and if he would be able to manage. My thoughts had been the same although there was nothing we really needed to cancel yet.

We didn't call Dr. Cuevas partly because Linda had an appointment for the next day and partly because we were afraid of what we might hear. She didn't make that appointment or the Forest Park Forever luncheon we had planned to attend. She still had a headache and she had no energy. She was also having great difficulty communicating. She needed a shower but didn't have enough strength for me to help her safely.

The next morning I called Dr. Cuevas' office to cancel the appointment and to update him. He said he would send a home health aide to help with the bathing. He wanted a little more time to review the options. The home health aide came late that afternoon. After seeing Linda and talking with us, she said she felt we would get more help from hospice. She would start the paperwork. She left without helping me give Linda a bath.

August 1, 2001

LINDA AND DAVE were married on August 1, 1992. It was a storybook wedding, at least to us. Linda was a beautiful bride and Dave was a handsome groom. Laura and the other bridesmaids all looked beautiful, too, with their bouquets of Stargazer lilies and teal dresses. Because the weather was exceptionally cool and dry for a St. Louis summer day, the hotel was able to serve the drinks and appetizers on an outdoor patio. Wedding pictures were taken on the hotel grounds where an abundance of impatiens added color. The bride and groom were appropriately toasted and everyone had a beautiful time.

Today was Linda and Dave's ninth wedding anniversary. Dave had made reservations for them to go to a popular area restaurant for dinner but it was apparent that Linda wouldn't be able to go. He cancelled the reservations and instead placed an order to bring the anniversary dinner home.

I thought hospice would be coming first thing in the morning but by mid-morning we still hadn't heard anything. I called Dr. Cuevas. He said he had reviewed the MRI and the tumor had grown. He agreed that hospice should begin. He also said to discontinue Gleevec. It wasn't working.

"How much has it grown since the last MRI?" I asked.

"It really doesn't matter," he said. "The tumor was so large already that any growth is bad."

At noon we still hadn't heard from hospice so I called them. They were waiting for the paperwork from Dr. Cuevas which they didn't expect to get until the next day because Dr. Cuevas wasn't in the office. Since I had just talked to Dr. Cuevas at another office, I gave them that phone number. Hospice called back to say that they could probably send someone late in the day to start the paperwork but it would be Thursday or Friday before they could send a hospice home health aide.

My patience and my emotions were ragged.

"Look!" I said, trying to keep my voice steady. "I don't care about the paperwork. It's my daughter's wedding anniversary and she hasn't had a bath since Friday. I just need someone to help me bathe her because she's too heavy for me to lift alone. She isn't a new patient for hospice anyway – we went through all the introductory paperwork in June."

The voice on the other end of the line at hospice heard my plea. Things started to happen pretty quickly then. Janet, a pleasant young woman, arrived within the hour. She would be Linda's home health aide. She gave Linda a bed bath and showed me what to do to help her. Feeling at least fresh and clean, Linda slept most of the afternoon. It was a relief to me, too. The supervising hospice nurse came late that afternoon to complete the paperwork. Debbie the nurse would be her regular nurse but she was on vacation this week.

Dave arrived home with the feast he had ordered – shrimp and steak and all the trimmings. Jared was with a friend and I was leaving so that Dave and Linda could have the evening alone. Linda, clean now and at least somewhat rested, came out to the family room as I was leaving. I will never forget how she looked. She sat limply in her wheelchair, groggy and a little disheveled, pale from illness – such a distant contrast from the young woman she had been.

"Happy Anniversary!" I said and kissed her goodbye – then left to cry my way home.

SANDY, THE SOCIAL worker from hospice, came the next day. Linda was sleeping but Sandy promised to talk to her in the next couple of weeks about what kind of funeral she wanted. As I suppose it is with many families going through this kind of long illness, funeral plans were something we could never really bring ourselves to discuss.

A hospice pastor also came because Pastor Paul, whom we'd met before, was on vacation. I also called Amy. I wanted to make sure she knew Linda was back on hospice care. Amy was going on vacation but would leave word with her secretary that she should be called if anything changed.

Janet, the health aide we had met earlier in the week, couldn't come on Friday so a different home health aide came. In the interim I had tried to give Linda a bed bath as best as I could, but it certainly didn't compare to what Janet was able to do. The new aide asked if Linda would prefer a shower.

"Yes," she shouted with tears coming down her face.

I looked at the aide and Nancy and Kay who were also there.

"Let's try it," I said. It took all four of us – a shower party of a different kind – but we did manage. Linda was overjoyed.

"Did you think you would never take another shower?" I joked. But we all knew that was a real possibility.

Linda's strength was declining so rapidly that it was getting increasingly difficult for me to help her with the essential transfers from the bed to the wheelchair and to the bathroom and back. Dave had enough brute strength that he could still manage but my back was starting to feel the strain. We had initially declined having a hospital bed – that just seemed too final. By the end of the week, a hospital bed was beginning to seem like a very good idea. I called hospice and they said a bed would be delivered on Saturday.

We had decided it would be easier for visitors and easier to monitor Linda if the bed were set up in the front of the house rather than the master bedroom. That afternoon I wheeled her through the family room and the front room so that she could decide where she wanted to have the bed. Neither one of us said what we were thinking. We both knew she was choosing the view she would have when she died.

Linda chose the front room which had plenty of light from a big window and a nice view down the street. Although the previous owners had used this room as a family room, she and Dave had set it up as a dining room. It was a large room, complete with a fireplace, bookshelves and a wet bar. The wet bar would be handy as a water source for us and the mantle served as a good place to store medications, out of reach of Jared.

On my way in that morning, I stopped and bought some single sheets and a lightweight summer blanket. I also bought some lamps, for the dining room table and chairs were the only furniture in the room. Dave and Linda hadn't had a chance yet to select a light fixture for over the dining room table.

We moved the dining room table to provide room for the bed. Photos, the albums we had picked up at school, flowers and cards and balloons soon collected on this table. The dining room chairs made it easy for visitors. Lamar added a plywood top to an old bathroom vanity we had been storing, making an improvised television stand at the foot of the bed. The vanity also provided useful storage.

Jared thought the hospital bed was pretty cool. He enjoyed showing his mommy how it cranked up and down and how easy it was for him to get up on it. He also thought it was pretty neat that Mommy had a big "kiki" – a thermal blanket made out of materials very similar to his favorite and slowly disintegrating blanket. He had fun demonstrating the controls and the blankets to visitors, too.

Although Mommy couldn't say so, I believe she thought the bed was pretty neat, too, it's flexibility allowing her to change positions more and to rest more comfortably. For the first few days she slept in the master bedroom with Dave at night. As she weakened, though, the hospital bed proved to be a more comfortable option and allowed Dave to get some rest.

On Monday the house was quiet after the hubbub of visitors during the weekend. I spent the day sitting next to Linda, reading a book called *Final Gifts*, written by Maggie Callahan and Patricia Kelley, both hospice people, about what it is like to die. Linda was sleeping most of the time and not eating or drinking much. Debbie the nurse told us these were all signs that the tumor was pretty aggressive – but then we already knew that. "Don't worry about her not eating or drinking much," Debbie said. "That's normal."

But how could I not worry?

I called Sandy the social worker to let her know that Linda seemed to be regressing quickly in terms of her ability to communicate. Perhaps she shouldn't wait too long to talk with Linda about funeral arrangements. We set the appointment for the next day.

That evening, Peggy, the hospice volunteer, stopped by to meet us. Lamar and Dave wheeled Linda's bed into the family room so she wouldn't seem quite so isolated. Peggy introduced herself to Linda and Jared and then sat and visited with us. I liked her immediately. If hospice had picked Sandy the social worker as a match for Dave and Linda, they had picked Peggy as a match for me. She was about my age and had lost her own son to cancer a few years before. I accompanied her to the door when it was time for her to leave. She turned and said, "Don't hesitate to call me if I can be of help!"

I appreciated her sensitivity – and did call her a few times.

Rachel was coming on Thursday. When I went home that night, I packed a few things so that I could stay overnight and help until Rachel got there.

August 7

THE DAY STARTED quietly. Linda rested comfortably all morning. Shortly before noon, her friend, Susan, stopped by with her little girl. She brought some tomatoes and banana peppers. She also brought some clothes for Jared that her son had never worn that she thought Jared might be able to use. Susan sat next to Linda's bed, visiting with her and holding her hand. When it came time for her to go she whispered softly, "Goodbye, girlfriend. I'll be back to see you."

Soon after Susan left, my friend Karla came bringing chocolate cake. With Karla's assistance, I was able to change the bed and give Linda a sponge bath.

Next came Sandy, the social worker. She visited with Linda for about half an hour while Karla and I had some lunch in the other room. When Sandy finished, she came to me to share what Linda had expressed as her wishes. Karla graciously offered to leave but I said it wasn't necessary.

Linda wanted a traditional funeral with a visitation and then a service at the funeral home, Sandy reported. This surprised me. I thought Linda would have preferred a funeral in a church but Sandy insisted that that was not what Linda wanted. I had many questions. No one in my immediate family had ever died before, nor had I ever been involved in planning or attending a funeral for anyone really close. I had already been living in Missouri when my grandparents died and that was before anyone flew anywhere.

Sandy made it very clear that it was Dave's responsibility to plan the funeral. If he asked me to participate, that was fine but ultimately the funeral was his responsibility. I could understand that but also hoped that I'd have some input. After all, Linda was our only child. Sandy suggested that one possibility would be to have the visitation for a couple of hours, followed immediately by the funeral. I bristled.

"I don't think two hours could possibly be long enough for all the people who will want to pay their respects," I told Sandy.

"It's not a wedding," she replied. "It's a funeral."

That I knew. But I also knew that my daughter was part of a larger community that would want to come. This visitation and this funeral should be a celebration of her life!

I hoped and prayed that Amy would return from her vacation before we had to worry about finalizing funeral arrangements.

Sandy left, saying she would call Dave about what she and Linda discussed. Before she went out the door, she leaned down and gave Linda a reassuring hug – a hug that Linda returned.

The visitors continued. Debbie, the nurse, came, followed by Janet, the home health aide. Janet managed to finish the bath I had started, making Linda feel much more comfortable.

Laura came and then Debbie, the teaching partner. Both of these young women had given Linda so much emotional support throughout this ordeal. Debbie was still with Linda when her next, and very special visitor came, Justin.

Justin and Linda had a very special student/teacher bond. He and his family had visited Linda in the hospital. He had been there for the walkathon and was one of the former students who had been interviewed for the television feature story, saying he would never forget her, she was a great teacher. He and his mother had sent many notes, cards, letters and pictures.

Justin arrived about 4:00 p.m. and only stayed for fifteen minutes or so. The fact that this high school student had the courage to come at all – and by himself – was a tribute to Linda. She was thrilled to see him. She had asked for a pain pill just before he came but had been unable to take it. Then I got an idea.

"OK," I said. "If you won't take your medicine for your mom, will you take it for Justin?"

And for Justin she did. This remarkable young man gave her a pill along with some tapioca pudding. Linda reached up with her good arm to give him a hug. It was a beautiful moment.

I wish the day had ended then.

W HEN DAVE CAME home from work each evening, he usually didn't say much more than a brief, "Hello!" He would then go out to the mailbox, bring the mail into the kitchen and start sorting through it. Until he was finished, it was hard to say much because that's where his attention was focused. This practice, normal as it might be under ordinary conditions, had become increasingly frustrating to me. If Linda could have talked more, it wouldn't have been necessary. But she couldn't.

Often there were things I felt Dave would want to know – events of the day or medical instructions before I started the drive home. The log helped but there were still some things easier to explain verbally. The longer it took for me to be able to convey the messages I thought he should hear, the later it would be before I got home. I'd never said anything about this to him but it bothered me just the same.

Linda was aware of my frustration. One day she was in the kitchen, in her wheelchair, when Dave started reading the mail. She looked at me, then looked at Dave, covering the mail with her hand and nodding in my direction. Dave listened then.

Today I was not driving home so it didn't matter. I was planning to spend the night. Lamar had driven in to join us for dinner. Linda was resting quietly and I had started supper. Jared was being picked up by a friend.

Dave came home, nodded "hello," deposited his briefcase and went out to get the mail. I waited, eager to tell him about

Justin and the other visitors and anxious to hear about his conversation with Sandy. He read his mail and took it back to the bedroom. He returned and opened his briefcase. He still had said hardly a word. Finally, I couldn't stand it anymore.

"Don't you want to hear about Linda's day?" I asked.

"I don't need to hear about her day," he said. "I know she's had a shitty day because of all the phone calls I've gotten at work!"

I lost it.

"She didn't have a 'shitty' day!" I shouted. "She actually had a very good day if you were willing to listen!"

Dave stormed off to the bedroom and I ran out of the house, screaming at the top of my lungs, "My only daughter is dying and I just can't take it anymore!"

Lamar followed me out.

"Get my keys!" I said. "I'm leaving."

"You're in no condition to drive."

"Get my keys! I'll go over to the Bierk's!"

Lamar went back in the house and returned with Dave. They both tried to talk some reason into me but I was too angry. We did go back in the house for a short while but I just had to get away. I drove to the Bierk's.

How much of this argument Linda heard I don't know. I hope she didn't hear it at all, but I will never know.

When I got to the Bierk's I was still shaking even after the short drive. We talked. Lamar arrived, too. When I had settled down enough I called hospice to let them know what had happened. I thought Dave might need some help and hoped someone could contact him. Debbie the nurse called and I explained the situation to her. She was a sympathetic listener but I'm sure she'd heard this kind of thing before.

Inside I was still raging and I was still hurt. My head was pounding and I was covered with hives – something I frequently get in reaction to stress. My ankles were swollen, too.

"I think I should check my blood pressure," I said, but the Bierks didn't have a gauge. Lamar offered to take me to the nearby emergency medical center and the Bierks convinced me to go. We arrived there a few minutes before closing but had a short wait before anyone could see us. When a nurse was finally able to check, my blood pressure had skyrocketed but I was pretty sure that the reading was already lower than it would have been earlier. The doctor gave me some nitroglycerin to help lower my blood pressure, told me to increase my blood pressure medication and we left to spend the night at the Bierk's.

That night I followed Debbie the nurse's suggestion and wrote a very long letter to Dave trying to explain why I'd gotten so angry. He had blown up with me before but this was the first time I had with him. The truth is, we were both hurting. We were both losing someone very precious and near and dear to us.

Nancy went over to Linda and Dave's early the next morning so that Dave could go to work. She delivered my letter. Lamar and I went over a little later. We hadn't been there long when Dave came home from work. He said he'd decided to work at home and set up his computer at the dining table in the front room where I was sitting next to Linda's bed.

"Do you want us to leave?" I asked.

"I have no problem if you stay," he said. That afternoon he left for an appointment and later went back to work. The afternoon visitors helped restore the more cheerful atmosphere we'd been trying to maintain for Linda's benefit.

The next day Rachel arrived. It was a relief to have her there. I enjoyed her company, she adored Linda and she loved and understood her son.

Together we would get through this.

WITH RACHEL THERE to help, I was able to stay home for a day – but just one. The hours and minutes we would still have to share with Linda were diminishing quickly.

Lamar and I arrived at the house at about 11:00 a.m. on Saturday morning. Cars lined the street in front of their house, looking auspiciously as if something had happened. Nothing had. It was just the houseful of family and visitors that were starting to congregate. Rick was there. One of Dave's brothers was there. Bridget and her daughter Tracy were there. And, of course, Linda was there.

Dave and Rachel were not there. In fact, Dave had called Bridget to help with Linda while he and Rachel went to the funeral home to make the preliminary arrangements. So, Dave was going to take Sandy at her word, I thought. He was going to do the planning himself without involving the mother-in-law. I felt strangely left out but Bridget's being there helped. She had found some Christmas lights in the basement. With Rick's help, she had strung them just outside the front window so Linda could see them from her bed. I was sure the lights were comforting to Linda, as she had always loved Christmas. OK. So we were having "Christmas" in August.

Dave and his mom had gone to Schrader's Funeral Home, the one Dave and I had discussed. When they returned after what seemed like forever, they shared the plans that had been made. These included visitation on one day with the funeral the next day in the large chapel at the home. I would still have a chance to choose flowers. The plans were fine – everything would work out and, hopefully, Amy would be back in town.

SUNDAY WAS A beautiful day – pleasantly warm rather than St. Louis's normal summer "hot." On the patio that morning, while Rachel stayed inside to watch Linda, Dave faced the formidable and unenviable task of telling Jared that Mommy would soon be going to join the angels. Jared had lots of questions, but I'm sure the session was much harder on Dave than it was on Jared.

Linda was more alert that afternoon and restless. "Would you like to go outside on the patio?" I asked.

She thought for a moment and nodded her head, "Yes."

Dave helped transfer her from the bed to the wheelchair. It took the combined strength of both Lamar and Dave to lift her wheelchair over the threshold and down the two small steps so as not to bump her unnecessarily.

Linda was outside again, if only for a moment, watching Jared play with his trucks in the mulch pile. It soon became apparent that she couldn't hold her head up on her own anymore. The stiffness in her neck forced her head down and to one side. Rachel and I alternated holding her hand and helping her hold her head up. Suddenly it seemed much warmer than it had been when I'd made the suggestion. All of us were perspiring.

"Would you like to go back inside?" I asked.

Again an affirmative nod. Dave and Lamar took her back inside for what would be the last time.

ON MONDAY, DEBBIE, the nurse, came again. She examined Linda in the very calming, reassuring way she had. When Linda was resting again, she shared with Rachel and me that she didn't think it would be much longer. Linda's skin color had changed. Debbie wouldn't commit to how much longer, though. "Soon," was all she would say. "Soon."

"Forget about any more solid food," she said. "Try jello and pudding."

As a mom, this was very hard to do. My instinct was to feed my child and to make sure she took her medicine. During the next few days we tried chocolate pudding, a previous favorite of Linda's, tapioca, jello, ice cream and even Kentucky Fried Chicken's mashed potatoes and gravy. She appeared to enjoy these but by mid-week we discovered that most of it was staying in her mouth – she couldn't swallow very well.

On Tuesday, Dave, Lamar and I went to the cemetery to pick out a plot. That seemed eerie, too – to be choosing a plot for someone so young who had been so vibrant and so full of life so recently. But it was something we had to do. Dave wanted to make sure that Linda would eventually have someone next to her, so Lamar and I were choosing our ultimate destination, too. We chose a simple gravesite that would have a flat stone and was in a quiet spot, near woods and away from the noise of the highway.

A steady stream of visitors continued during the week. A lot of Linda's waking time was spent trying to give her food and medicine – particularly the seizure control medicine. She still hadn't needed much pain medicine but that changed quickly, too. By Thursday, Debbie said not to worry about any other medicine except for the pain medicine and changed that to liquid form.

It was eerie. I felt like we were starving her to death – or at the very least, attributing to dehydration. This was especially true when she was awake and alert. But then she would try to move her head and couldn't, or she would hold her head from tumor headache pain. Keeping her as comfortable as possible was all we could do.

I saw the reason now for the high-topped tennis shoes Linda had worn on the ninth floor of the hospital to keep her feet straight – avoiding "ankle-drop" I think they called it. Now, after just a few consecutive bed-ridden days, her feet were curling forward. I stood at the end of her bed, rubbing her feet, as I chatted with visitors.

Rachel called her school in Illinois to say she wouldn't be there on Monday, the first day of school for her students. She just couldn't leave now. The school was very understanding.

August 17

PEGGY, THE HOSPICE volunteer, came by the house. She sat next to Linda's bed as she paged through some of the many photo albums we had gathered in the room – family albums, Jared albums and the albums of each class that Linda had made. (Photos of this year's class were still in a box on the table, waiting.)

Peggy had only been there a short time when the doorbell rang. It was Grace, Linda's kindergarten teacher and a colleague and friend of mine for many years. She had had lunch with my friend Jan and had just learned about Linda. Grace brought with her that special expertise that kindergarten teachers have to ease your hurt and pain and make you laugh instead of cry.

We – Peggy, Grace, Linda and, from time to time, Rachel – visited for a long time, sharing stories about Linda as a little girl, Linda growing up, her beautiful wedding, her teaching, Jared. Linda was awake for most of Grace's visit, raising her eyebrow and nodding slightly in agreement or disagreement as we reminisced.

It was incredibly comforting.

THAT AFTERNOON, JANET came to give Linda another bed bath. Visitors came in and out all afternoon, too. Something seemed to be bothering Linda but we couldn't figure out what it was. We tried this and then that, any little thing we could do to make her more comfortable but nothing seemed to work quite right.

When I arrived the next morning, I noticed how Linda's color had faded – something hospice had warned us would happen. Linda was still restless and seemed uncomfortable. Kay returned from her vacation and came over right away. We needed her. With Kay's help and a call to Debbie at hospice, we learned Linda had developed a urinary infection. Debbie was on call for the weekend so came to help remove the catheter. With this irritant removed, Linda was able to rest and to sleep even with the many visitors that continued throughout the day.

Lamar and I had a dinner invitation for that evening but I was reluctant to leave. By the end of the afternoon, Linda had perked up some. And she was in good hands. Rachel and Dave were both there and plenty of other people would be around to help if needed. So I gave Linda a hug and she reached up to stroke my hair, letting me know it was all right to go. I left, promising to call later that evening. When I did call, Rachel reported that Linda had asked for the oxygen but seemed to be sleeping comfortably.

I decided to stay home and drive back in the morning.

August 19, 2001

I WAS AWAKE early and rushed to get ready to leave. I felt guilty about not having gone back to Linda's to spend the night but Rachel had reassured me that everything seemed to be OK. Linda was sleeping when I called in the morning to check. Lamar was finishing up some outside chores and then would drive in separately.

"Don't wait too long to come!" I called to him as I rushed out of the house.

Linda was still sleeping when I got there. Dave and Jared had gone to church. Rachel was trying to catch up on some sleep on the couch. The house was quiet as I sat by Linda, reading the paper some but watching her sleep more. Her eyes didn't open nor did she seem to know that I was there. Nancy arrived to join the vigil shortly before Dave and Jared returned from church.

Suddenly Linda's eyes opened slightly but only for a moment. They didn't seem to focus on anything in particular. I gave one look at Nancy and then called Dave and Rachel from the kitchen. The time had come.

We quickly surrounded Linda's bed, Dave holding Jared in his lap. Dave kissed her hand and vowed to take good care of Jared. We all held her tightly and prayed as she took a few last gasps of breath.

Soon Linda had joined her beloved angels.

Within moments of Linda's death, we looked out the window and saw Anna, one of Linda's students, coming up the front walk with her mother and younger brother. They were bringing dinner for that evening. I rushed out the door to meet them before they could ring the doorbell.

"She's gone," I said, "just a few minutes ago."

Their faces mirrored my anguish as I accepted their hugs and the food and made Anna and her brother promise that they would do their very best in school this coming year. "That's what Linda would want you to do," I said.

Dave called hospice and the priest. He also called the funeral home. I called Manchester Methodist hoping they would get the message to Amy who was due back from vacation that day.

Bridget arrived. Then Lamar.

Earlier I had tried unsuccessfully to reach Lamar by cell phone to tell him to hurry. The others had left the front room where Linda still lay so that he and I could go in and say our good-byes, but it took some coaxing. He wasn't sure he wanted to see her this way. But he did, just for a few minutes.

The long struggle was over.

Linda Update, August 19

LINDA REBECCA KARLOVETZ Favero passed away this morning at 11:00 a.m. She was resting peacefully and all of us were with her.

She died on the same day and at almost exactly the same time as she and Dave were to leave on their trip to Oregon. She had said she wanted to go somewhere that she had never been and she got her wish – but to a better destination.

Visitation will be held on Wednesday, August 22, from 3:00 p.m. to 9:00 p.m. – Linda's thirty-third birthday.

Funeral services will be held on Thursday, August 23, the first day of school.

I am reminded of second-grader Mara's beautiful poem, "The Classroom is Bare."

Yes, Linda's classroom is bare but she has taught us all so much. May she rest in peace.

Martha

Linda Rebecca Favero,
August 22, 1968 - August 19, 2001

Chapter 9

Linda's Legacy

August 22, 2001

THIS WAS LINDA'S BIRTHDAY. SHE would have been thirty-three today. We should have been having a party. Instead, we were having a wake.

The past two days were a blur of making final arrangements. Amy was back in town and would be officiating at the funeral along with the young priest. Lamar and I joined Rachel and Dave to work out the details at the funeral home. The large reception room and the chapel were both available at the times we needed them. My brothers and sisters-in-law and my father were flying in to be here. Dave's family was on its way from Illinois and California. We had friends from California coming too.

A special group of Mason Ridge parents were making the arrangements for food following the ceremony. Bridget, aided by some other parents, worked with the kids in Linda's class to make a photo album of their two years as her students. Linda had carefully made albums for each of the year's she had taught except for this very last class. The photos had been sitting on the dining room table, waiting for someone to put them together. No one could have done a better job with the album than these students did.

Those of us in the immediate family arrived at the funeral home early even though the wake wouldn't begin for another two hours. The funeral home suggested this so we would have some private time with Linda. Amy, or I should say, Pastor Amy as she was now in her full, professional role, came and gave a blessing. We then had some time to add our personal touches to the room and to admire the flowers that were still arriving.

The long reception room where the wake was to be held was more like an oversized living room than a funeral parlor. We were able to scatter photos of Linda and family on tables in conversation areas throughout the room, almost as if she had lived there. The picture of Linda as a beautiful young bride took a prominent spot. So did a family photo of Lamar, Dave, Linda and I taken before Jared was born. And there was the very special photo of Linda and Jared together that she had had taken for Mother's Day the year Jared was three.

At one end of the huge room we set up a "classroom" area, the mementos of her life as a teacher and of her students. The photo albums she had made for each class and the one this year's students had just completed were on one table. Other photos were posted on a nearby bulletin board. The tall director's chair and the beautifully painted wooden chair that classes had presented to her were there, too. So was the huge, three-foot pencil presented to her class at the time of the D.A.R.E. award and the ceramic plates, gifts from other classes.

Then there were the mementos of her long illness – the scrapbook that Linda and I had compiled of cards and letters from students and parents, the huge poster from the walkathon in her honor and some of the many stuffed animals that had been sent to comfort her.

Flowers and plants filled every other nook in the room and towered in a semi-circle around the casket where Linda lay. Dave had helped Jared place a small teddy bear angel next to Linda's shoulders, right below the small bouquet of flowers that were from him. She looked beautiful. And she looked at peace.

The receiving line began to form before the doors were opened. Dave stood on one side of the casket and I on the other as we greeted the hundreds of people that came to pay their respects. Lamar stayed near the beginning of the line, greeting people who decided not to wait in the long line.

Dave's coworkers and neighbors and college friends were there, some of the latter with children in infant seats. Friends of ours, both new and old, including some people we'd lost touch with, came to share our sorrow. There were people we barely knew but who had known Linda and wanted to be there.

Dr. Butler and Dr. Rosenfeld came. They had certainly done all they could, medically, to save her. Along the way Linda had earned a special place in their memories for her indomitable spirit and determination. Trish and Barb and Laura were there from rehab as well. These three young women were all close to Linda in age, had identified with her and treated Linda's struggle as their own. A patient who had been in rehab at the same time as Linda came, saying how much she had admired Linda's courage.

There were teachers – lots of them – teachers who had worked with Linda, teachers who were colleagues of mine and teachers who knew us both. And there were Jared's teachers from Love and Laughter who had given him so much support over the last year.

But most special of all were the students, past and present, who came to pay tribute to this teacher they loved. They poured over the albums and scrapbooks and waited patiently in line. Some were with their parents, some by themselves. Dave and I both had a very similar message for these students, a message that Linda would have given them if she had been able to: "Do your very best in school this year! That's what Mrs. Favero would want you to do."

The receiving line did not diminish until the very end, late in the evening. While I took one short break to visit with out-of-town guests who had assembled in a small reception room downstairs, Dave stood there for the entire six hours, a final act of courage, support and love for Linda, his college sweetheart.

EARLY THE NEXT morning, I wrote to my mother whose health made travel impossible. I knew that she was with us in spirit.

Aug. 23, 2001

> *Dear Moo:* (my nickname for my mother)
> You would have been very proud of your granddaughter yesterday. What would have been her thirty-third birthday turned out to be a wonderful tribute and celebration of her life.
> From 1:30 p.m. to 3:00 p.m., Lamar and I, Dave and his family had time to see Linda – beautiful as she lay in peace, admire the incredible flowers, and put out some memorabilia.
> At 3:00 p.m. the doors opened to visitors. The line was already waiting at the door. For the next six hours there was a long line of people – friends, teachers, students (both former and current) and others who patiently waited to pay their respects and to pay tribute to her.
> Two very special things had been delivered to the funeral home to honor Linda. One was a beautiful photo album made by the fifth grade students she loved so much. In it they share their memories of a wonderful teacher. The second was a Missouri Senate Proclamation passed in her honor.
> I mourn but I cannot feel sad. Linda contributed so much in her short life that her legacy will go on forever. She left a lesson for all her teaching colleagues: teachers do make a difference in the lives of every child they touch. She left a lesson for all of us about courage and strength.
> Thank you for being my mother – you inspired me. Thank you for being Linda's grandma. You inspired her to be what she was.
> *Love, Til* (my mother's nickname for me)

August 23, 2001

TODAY WAS THE first day of school. Students and teachers throughout the St. Louis area were returning after the summer break. Everyone, that is, except for one very special teacher.

Did Linda plan the time she died? It seemed so. First, the moment of her death coincided almost precisely with the departure time of the trip she and Dave had planned. Visitation was on her birthday, the day before school started so students and teachers could come without interrupting that important first day of the year. And, because the funeral was going to be held on the first day of school, the lovely chapel at the funeral home would be better able to accommodate those who could attend.

We arrived early again and waited in a room set aside for the family. It was a hushed gathering as Pastor Amy and the priest spoke with us. Even Jared was quiet, sensing the importance of this occasion and probably feeling a little uncomfortable in the smart little suit jacket a friend had given him. His eyes were red but I don't think it was from crying, just simply lack of sleep. Laura and Debbie and Todd and Mark joined us. They were pallbearers along with Dave's brothers and brother-in-law. Linda would have liked that. My friend, Jan, was there, too. Much to my surprise – and hers – Dave had asked her to be one of the witnesses at the service. Linda would have liked that, too.

The chapel and the adjacent overflow room were filled to capacity as we entered and were escorted to the first few rows reserved for the family. Dave and Jared led the procession, followed by his parents, then Lamar and me. From where I was sitting I could see Justin and Tracey and their moms, Ruth and Bridget, sitting in the front row of the overflow room. Linda would have felt honored – and even a little embarrassed – that attending this service was more important in their lives than the first day of school. She also would have gently chastised them.

At my request the organist opened the service with "Fourteen Angels" from the opera, *Hansel and Gretel*. I'm not sure anyone else in the audience detected the significance of this music but it didn't matter. I was singing noiselessly along with the music, improvising the words as Linda and I had always done when I tucked her in at night as a little girl.

The service had barely begun when Jared starting getting restless and tiptoed across the front row to me. I gathered him into my arms and held him closely. He quickly fell asleep. Throughout the beautiful service I could look up at the now closed casket surrounded by flowers and then down at the beautiful child sleeping in my arms, the little boy who so much resembled his mother. If Jared had wanted to choose a way to comfort his grandma, his mommy's mommy, he couldn't have chosen a better way.

The priest spoke first. He had not met Linda until after her death but even in that short time had learned much about her spirit. He quoted Paul's letter to the *Corinthians* about love (1 Cor. 13:4-8):

> *Love is patient and kind.*
> *Love is not jealous or boastful or arrogant or rude.*
> *Love does not insist on its own way; it is not irritable or resentful.*
> *Love does not rejoice in the wrong but rejoices in the truth.*
> *Love bears all things, believes all things, hopes all things, endures all things.*
> *Love never ends.*

DAVE MAY HAVE suggested the passage but did the priest know that Linda had often cross-stitched these same words onto samplers she made as wedding gifts for friends that were getting married? I don't think so. He reminded us of Linda's love for teaching and love of life and challenged us to make that memory real . . . to live on in her love.

A soloist sang a beautiful rendition of *Ave Maria* and then it was Pastor Amy's turn. She read from the scripture (*John 13:14*), telling about Jesus as a "master teacher," the vision he had given his disciples and the gift of comfort he had also given them. Amy spoke about the two times in Linda's life journey that she had known Linda, first as a high school student and a young college student at Illinois Wesleyan; later as a young mother, parent, wife, teacher and an adult woman living with cancer. Amy continued:

IN BOTH OF those journey times of her life, in which I had the privilege of knowing my friend, Linda, I experienced someone who was living in the light of the Master Teacher. Especially in these past months, these months that for many of us might have seemed hopeless and helpless as we were looking in on Linda's life, I saw her giving to us and her family and to Jared and to all those around her those very same gifts that the Master Teacher Jesus gave to his disciples in that Upper Room, I saw her giving to her family and friends the vision and expectation and hope that life will go on. . . . She didn't let us shut down in our work but she had a hope and an expectation that we would continue as the teachers that we are, whether that be in our home or in our work places or in our schools.

But I also saw Linda giving that very same gift of the Master Teacher in compassion and care. If you had been with someone and journeyed with someone as closely as David and Jared and her family have been with Linda, you know how easy it would be to shut persons out of a journey of dying. How easy it would be to let persons stay at a distance and not get close on this very painful journey. But Linda chose to live with dying differently. She chose to give us the gift of the Master Teacher of care and compassion by inviting us into her journey and in an amazing and graceful way, Linda did some of her best teaching in her dying.

AMY COMPLETED THIS analogy and then gave the traditional biography. But she shared the information about Linda's life with such joy in her voice and her expression, many people would comment about it later. She concluded by saying Linda was a cherished child of God and thanked God for sharing her with us, allowing our life journeys to be blessed because of her presence in our lives.

My brother Dave, Linda's uncle, was next. He is a writer by trade and had written many poems and odes and satires for family events. While this ode may not have been the most difficult one he ever had to write, I'm sure it was the hardest one he ever had to deliver.

Ode to Linda
A Supernatural Teacher

Have you ever come upon a sight in the natural world that left you in awe, speechless, unable to think or talk or even breathe? A towering waterfall breaking through the mist, perhaps, or a stunning sunset, fiery orange ball slipping slowly behind dark distant mountains. A loon landing on a still morning lake. Moonbeams rippling over ocean waves. A baby's first cry.

Have you ever had a teacher whose lessons you still remembered long after that final bell signaled the end of a class or a year? It wasn't just what she said or what he did, that teacher. It was how you are you because of the way that teacher was. It wasn't just the way that teacher held things up to the light and made you want to know more about them. It was the way that teacher loved you enough to open your heart.

I've reveled in such sights in nature. And I've had such teachers, rare gems though they be. But never before have I encountered a teacher whose love of life, whose lessons of spirit, left me so in awe, like the sight of the loon or the moon, the sound of the waterfall or the baby's call.

Until I witnessed the teacher whose life and lessons we celebrate here today. Until I felt the beauty and the power of Linda Rebecca Karlovetz Favero as she fought her last battle, as she taught her last class.

Linda did not lose her battle against that tumor. She won. She won because of the way she lived her life and the way she met her death.

So let's celebrate Linda's victory and remember the lessons she taught each one of us.

Let's start with just a few excerpts from some of the scores and scores of letters Linda received from current and former students for their thanks and appreciation.

From Justin: "You taught me that someone can do whatever they want, even under the hardest circumstances. You have made a great difference here. A good difference. I will never forget you."

From Katelyn: "When I was in your class, you touched me like no one else could. I felt like an individual among my peers and I know they did as well. What was most important, though, is that you gave me a sense of passion."

FROM LAURA LIBERMAN, in her sterling poem, *My Hero*:

"The days passed and my school days with you ended
. . that was not the end.
No, I had more unfinished business needing attention.
Seeing the baby, helping with your room.
Those were all the decoys, so that I could be with you.
Having fun times as I saw the world in a new view."

FROM A CONGRATULATORY note from the Mason Ridge PTO at the time of Linda's Teacher of the Year recognition:
"You have taught our children how to read and write. You have taught all of us strength, courage, determination and respect! We love you and thank you for being the incredible person that you are."

ALLOW ME NOW to share a short story that, for me, in an ordinary way, captures the extraordinary spirit and profound wisdom of this supernatural teacher.

Just over a month ago, my brother Tony, my wife Tina and I spent a weekend at Martha and Lamar's house on the lake. We were sitting at the breakfast table early in the morning. Suddenly, Linda turned and maneuvered her wheelchair over to the corner cupboard. She opened the cupboard with her one good hand. And searched the cupboard for something, we knew not what. Martha came over to see if she could help. It was finally determined, after many questions and shakings of heads, that she wanted Martha to take from the cupboard a package of cookies, Vienna Fingers to be precise. Which Martha did. "Do you want Vienna Fingers for breakfast?" Martha asked Linda, puzzled. Linda shook her head, "No." More questions, more negative responses. Finally, Linda nodded towards me. She had remembered that I love Vienna Fingers and have a tendency to devour them by the handful. She had made sure, prior to our visit, that she had purchased a package of Vienna Fingers and that that package of Vienna Fingers had been transported from her house to Martha and Lamar's house. And then from the cupboard to the table and then to her uncle's mouth.

So, there you have it. This courageous young women who had endured countless sessions of therapy with no quit in her bones and withstood untold hours of pain with no complaint in her soul; this mother who could no longer do everything for her son, her Jared, that a mother yearns to do; this teacher who could no longer be in the classroom with the students she loved doing what she loved most to do had invested some of her precious waning energy store to make sure her Uncle Dave got his Vienna Fingers.

Linda Favero needed no blackboard or chalk to convey life's lessons. She could do so with cookies – at a table on a Saturday morning in a house by a lake. She could do so with a smile. Or a twinkle in the eye. Or, at her wedding, by putting a spoon on her nose. She could do so because she had a natural gift for lighting up any room when she walked through any door.

I'd like to close with a poem by Mara Lesser, a second grader and sister of fifth grader, Ben.

The Classroom is Bare

The classroom is bare because the teacher is not there.
When the teacher is not there the classroom is bare.
The children sit at their desk alone, working and working
as hard as they should.
So, they work and work until the teacher comes back.
Day after day they work very hard.
One day the teacher comes back to teaching
with joy and happiness.
She is a great teacher.
The classroom is not bare anymore and we are all
happy because Mrs. Favero is back.
I miss her very much.

Mara Lesser

LET ME SAY to you, Mara, that we all miss Linda Favero very much. But, when you really think about it, Linda's classroom is not bare at all. It's very full. Because Linda's classroom was the world of people around her, wherever she went. She shared her light with us every day in every way. And now, if we remember her lessons, we share that light with others which gives them, in turn, more light to pass on. If we face tough battles, even those we are destined to lose, we follow Linda's example; we never ever give up and other people see our courage which gives them courage and so it goes, and on and on.

Can't you see, then, Mara, the ripple effect created by the life lessons of this daughter, wife, mother, niece, cousin, friend? Isn't it a wonder? Isn't it like magic? Isn't it just what you would expect from Linda Rebecca Karlovetz Favero, a supernatural teacher?

What a gift she was.
What a gift she is.
What a gift she will continue to be.
What a gift!

THEN IT WAS Jan's turn.

Students remember their teachers... and teachers remember their students.

LINDA IS REMEMBERED by her kindergarten teacher, Grace Phillips, as a bright five-year old little girl. She was bright not only in the intelligent sort of way, but also bright in spirit and enthusiasm, an eager learner and a happy student and a beautiful little girl – although Linda was very talkative. Grace remembered Linda's father, Lamar, as a special part of Linda's life. And parent teacher conferences were memorable because Linda's mother, Martha, always showed up with a homemade gift, preserves or cookies. When Linda grew up, she and Martha would bake wonderful Christmas cookies and many of us were recipients of Linda's baked goods. Late night or middle of the night baking sessions became Linda's way of handling times when she couldn't sleep.

It seems only fitting that Linda became a master teacher. After all, she had a great role model: her mom. She grew up immersed in the profession of teaching and often tolerating her mother's teacher friends! But like her mother, Linda, was a strong, independent-minded woman. She earned the respect of her colleagues, and the devotion of her students. She was a true professional and a dedicated teacher. Like her mother, she had begun to involve herself in her local teachers' association, and Linda wasn't shy about standing up for what she believed in. But she was her own person on her own terms – as Linda Favero, not as Martha's daughter. She followed in Martha's footsteps, but never in her shadow.

Linda and her dad had a very special bond. Lamar was an important player in Linda's early years and she truly enjoyed spending time with him. Although she wasn't above teasing him, or playing an occasional prank, she adored Lamar and she could often wrap him around her little finger. She was thrilled when she and Dave could give him a grandson.

So, I guess you could say Linda was her Mother's daughter and her Daddy's girl.

And then there was one weekend when she brought this fella home from college. Dave had to pass inspection first by mom and dad and then by her "second" family, Nancy, Jack and of course Todd and Mark. We all saw that Dave was a keeper! And as an only child, Linda was delighted to be a part of Dave's big family.

Last week I saw the memorial service for Maureen Reagan, who also lost her battle with cancer, her friend David Hyde Pierce proclaimed "When life gave Maureen lemons—she just threw them right back!" I laughed to myself and thought, "He should meet Linda!"

Linda wasn't only a teacher of children. She taught her friends and family each and everyday. She was our role model. We looked to her as she fought this indiscriminate disease and we learned about dignity, honesty, strength and humor. I know those last days she was at peace. She was surrounded by friends and family, the memory of a breeze on her face as she took a last boat ride across the lake, a stroke of the hair of someone she loved and feeling the last, loving touch of a kiss.

THE WORDS OF poet Isla Richardson speak for Linda:

To Those I Love

If I should ever leave you whom I love,
To go along the Silent Way,
Grieve not, nor speak of me with tears,
But laugh and talk of me as if I were beside you,
For who knows, but that I shall be oftentimes?
I'd come, I'd come could I but find a way!
But would not tears and grief be barriers?
And when you hear a song I used to sing,
Or see a bird I loved – let not the thought of me be sad,
For I am loving you just as I always have…
You were so good to me…
So many things I wanted still to do…
So many, many things to say to you…
Remember that I did not fear…
It was just leaving you I could not bear to face…
We cannot see beyond….
But this I know; I loved you so–
'twas heaven here with you!

FINALLY IT WAS Dave's turn. He took a very deep breath and began:

Dear Linda:
OVER THE LAST two days Jared and I have had the opportunity to gather with family, friends and students to pay our respects and celebrate your life. It is obvious based on the outpouring of emotion and support that your presence has made an incredible impression both inside and outside the classroom. You have made both of us very proud.

It is amazing to think back almost seven years and remember the day we learned of your cancer. I can remember one of the doctors saying, "No teaching! No children!" These were just a couple of the "nos." At the time we were both crushed and certainly unsure of the journey on which we were about to embark. In my opinion, that journey was one hell of a ride. Think about it: a Caribbean cruise, trips to Florida, Maine, New York, San Francisco and Wisconsin; professional accomplishments such as Missouri D.A.R.E. Teacher of the Year, Forest Park Forever, zoo overnights and Mason Ridge Teacher of the Year. And finally, and certainly most important of all, our son Jared, all of this while battling cancer.

Your physical and mental strength is unbelievable. I often wondered how you were able to sustain such a positive attitude in the face of such adversity. Hindsight: I believe you lived with a sense of urgency but maintained a true appreciation for life. Your approach towards life, your openness regarding your cancer, your ability to teach and your communication skills provided the foundation from which young and old could learn. Classroom lessons in combination with your life experiences that you shared with both young and old have provided wonderful examples of unselfishness, humility, courage, commitment, determination and perseverance.

Speaking for Jared and me, we are better human beings because of our experiences with you. Over the last eight months it has been very difficult for Jared and me to watch the woman we love go through so many peaks and valleys. One thing that we are thankful for is the fact that you had the time to experience the appreciation and love others developed for you as a result of what you had done for them. It has been wonderful to be a part of that.

In closing, the time that you, Jared and I had together has been cut short. But I do know one thing for sure, we'll love you forever, we'll like you for always, as long as we're living our inspiration you'll be. You'll be in our hearts forever.

Love, David and Jared

Although Dave struggled to get through some parts of it, he made it. Perhaps because the entire audience – and Linda – was silently cheering him on. The service concluded with a solo and then all of us joining in to sing.

Let There be Peace on Earth

Let there be peace on earth and let it begin with me;
Let there be peace on earth, the peace that was meant to be.
With God our creator, children all are we,
Let us walk with each other in perfect harmony.
Let peace begin with me, let this be the moment now;
With every step I take, let this be my solemn vow:
To keep each moment and live each moment in peace eternally.
Let there be peace on earth and let it begin with me.

LINDA WOULD HAVE been pleased.

Afterword

August 22, 2002

TODAY WOULD HAVE BEEN LINDA'S thirty-fourth birthday. She would have had her own classroom ready and stayed home just a little longer to see Jared off for that exciting first day of kindergarten. But she wasn't here to do that.

Instead, Lamar and I drove in early in the morning to meet Dave and Jared at their house. We posed for pictures outside the house before driving the short distance to the school. Jared was proudly sporting the new backpack that he had personally selected. Fully loaded with supplies, the pack was almost as big as he was.

This was actually Jared's third trip to the school for the week. Even so, while lying in bed the night before he had called out to his daddy to say that if he was going to ride his bike to school (which he wasn't), he would need a map. Two days earlier I had taken him to a bus orientation program for kindergartners. We had met his teacher and had seen his classroom. The evening before, I had joined Dave and Jared for an open house the school hosts the day before the first day of school. This unique event gives students and parents the opportunity to find their classrooms and meet their teachers, greatly reducing first day jitters. Parents also have the opportunity to sign up to help with their child's class and pay any fees, saving teachers from some of the paperwork overload of the first few weeks of school.

Jared entered the "latch-key" area where he will normally begin his school day somewhat timidly, the three of us following. By the time we had gotten to the main part of the building, some familiar sights bolstered his confidence. He motioned for us to come and led us across the multi-purpose room to his classroom. Minutes after his teacher showed him where to put his backpack and he gave us quick kisses and hugs, he joined a group of his classmates in a game on the floor. We could go now, he seemed to be saying, he would be just fine. After all, he wasn't new to a school setting, just to this particular school.

Lamar and I saw Dave off to work and then headed for the cemetery where Linda is buried. I'd brought a wreath of silk Stargazer lilies that Nancy had helped me make the night before. The wreath added some color next to the small, flat stone engraved with an angel. Nearby, in front of a recently planted crab apple tree, is a commemorative marker showing that the tree is a gift in the memory of Linda Favero from the staff of Pierremont School. In the early morning hours the sun hasn't yet made it over the crest of the hill, so the grave is in cool shade. Very quiet, very peaceful and, yes, very sad.

We left to go grocery shopping and to run errands and to do all the mundane things we do in our everyday lives, but we are silent as we drive away. It's not that we haven't adjusted to life without Linda. I think we have. It's just that some days and some circumstances are harder than others. Ironically, the first week of school, Linda's birthday and the anniversary of her death will always coincide.

IN OCTOBER FOLLOWING Linda's death, Lamar and I took a trip to Canada and New England for the fall foliage. We traveled at a leisurely pace, staying in quaint B&Bs, and enjoying the spectacle of color that New England offers at that time of year. It was beautiful and helped us forget – well, not quite. At a lovely candlelit dinner one night, complete with classical music playing softly in the background, I began to cry for no real reason at all, my emotions still very close to the surface.

The New England trip was a long vacation detour towards a trip to Manlius, New York, outside of Syracuse. My brothers, cousins and I had planned a pre-ninetieth birthday celebration for my mother. Her birthday was actually not until January 3 but Syracuse winter weather makes travel iffy at best so we'd set the date for mid-October. Even though I knew from regular phone calls that my mother's health had declined, I was startled to see just how much she had aged. It had been almost a year since I had seen her and she didn't recognize me when I first walked into her room.

My mother rallied for the intergenerational party we held in the assisted living residence's small dining room and enjoyed it thoroughly. When we said our good-byes the next morning I felt certain that I would probably not see her alive again. Two weeks later she passed away, too quickly for me to be with her but in time to contact some friends of hers. I was in the St. Louis airport waiting to board a plane to Syracuse when I received the call on my cell phone telling me she had passed away. I continued on my journey anyway to help make the final arrangements and dismantle my mother's small apartment. My brother, Anthony, was there to help, too, as my other brother, Dave, had a work commitment.

In December, I made one more trip to Syracuse for a beautiful memorial service planned by the RAFFA group, a non-denominational church without walls whose members had been my mother's Syracuse support group for over thirty years.

How glad we all were that we had celebrated her ninetieth birthday early!

OUR CONTACT WITH Dave and Jared has not been as constant as it had been when Linda was ill, but we do see them frequently. They both came to our house for Lamar's birthday in September. Jared helped me make the cake. Lamar and I took Jared to the zoo. I took him to *Disney on Ice* – along with Laura and her little boy and Bridget and her youngest daughter. We are always glad when Dave calls on us to help out by taking Jared for a weekend stay that also gives him a break.

Dave discovered from one of the subdivision trustees that the large side yard of their house had been the traditional gathering place for the young families in the neighborhood to have a hot dog roast before going Trick or Treating. He invited us in to join the party. Jared and I carved pumpkins – three of them – the weekend before. He was a rambunctious Spider Man, his costume of choice, for Halloween. But I felt like Mother Hubbard without a costume at the party. The group was the next generation of parents with young children and one parent, Linda, wasn't there. I felt prematurely old. When Dave and Jared left for Jared to do his own Halloween tour of the neighborhood, a wave of nostalgia engulfed me. I stifled the tears so that I could greet the children who came to the door for their treats cheerfully.

Dave and Jared were obviously going through their adjustment period, too. The house must have been incredibly lonely after the hustle and bustle of those last few weeks. In fact, Dave told me that Jared had asked one day on the way home from pre-school who was going to be there when they got home. "Just us," Dave had replied. "Just us."

Dave and Jared joined a support group for parents and children but Dave wasn't convinced that it was that effective. After several weeks in attendance, he asked the facilitator who worked with the children if she had any insights as to how Jared was adjusting. She really couldn't comment on anything specifically. After the first of the year Dave switched to a private child psychologist. This, I think, helped Jared and helped give Dave some guidance as a single parent adjusting to his own loss.

At first Jared would not talk about his mommy at all. If I mentioned her he would say, "Don't talk about my mommy. She's dead!"

Now, he is beginning to talk about his mother more, to ask questions or to say, "I used to do that with my mommy." By special request, we even made Linda's famous poppy seed bread because that was something he remembered doing with his mommy.

WE KNEW THAT Christmas would be bittersweet. My brother, Dave, his wife, Tina and my father were coming to help us get over the hurdle that this first Christmas holiday would be. I looked forward to having them here, to decorating and cooking again, and to our traditional celebration with the Bierks.

Christmas baking together had been a long-established tradition for Linda and me. For my sixtieth birthday she had made a recipe notebook for each of us of all the recipes we had made over the years – some tried and true old favorites along with the new ones we would add each year. Debbie, Linda's teaching partner, had suggested that some of the teachers from Mason Ridge would like to get together to bake cookies and offered to host the party at her house.

The First Annual Linda Cookie Bake was held at Debbie's house on a Saturday early in December. I had printed out our recipes and apportioned out ingredients to bring to a dozen people, teachers and Laura and Nancy. We had cookie dough and cookies scattered throughout Debbie's house and even on the porch outside as it was an unseasonably warm day. A few hours and lots of laughter and memories of Linda later, each baker left for home with a few dozen cookies.

I continued to make cookies – and poppy seed bread. A few days before the holiday, I repeated a tradition Linda had established. I delivered some of these goodies to St. Luke's hospital – to the rehab department and to radiation oncology. I was doing fine until Dr. Butler came out to offer his own thanks and ask how we were all doing. Sometimes grief hits you when you least expect it.

Dave and Jared arrived at our house on December 22, loaded down with presents, just before dinnertime. I had just finished getting ready and had turned on the Christmas lights, started Christmas music and lit the candles. Lamar had gone to pick up my family at the airport. Unfortunately their plane was almost two hours late!

Those two hours were the longest two hours of Christmas I have ever had. Jared was hungry and eager to begin festivities. Dave and I tried a couple of times to make small conversation but neither of us felt much like it. The candlelit atmosphere of the room brought back too many memories of happier times. We spent most of that time in our own reverie while Jared entertained himself on the computer. I am sure it was just as much a relief for Dave as it was for me when the clan finally arrived from the airport.

The Bierk party was the next night. We could have turned back the clock one year except Linda was not among us. The excitement and scuffles of three young boys: Jared and the Bierks' grandsons, Connor and Clay, still made for a festive occasion. On Christmas Eve morning Dave and Jared drove to Lockport, Illinois to celebrate Christmas with his family.

For some time, I had planned to attend the Christmas Eve service at Manchester Methodist, weather permitting, even though it was a very long drive. On the way, I wanted to place some luminary candles that I had made on Linda's grave. The rest of the family joined me. When we arrived at the cemetery it was still daylight and very windy. The dirt over her grave had settled, staring up at us in cold clay clods. We lit the luminary candles and hoped they'd survive the crush of blasting wind.

We had chosen the early 5:00 p.m. family service because of the distance we had to drive, but perhaps someone above had helped us make that decision. Linda's friend and minister, Pastor Amy, led this service. Amy exchanged the ministerial robe she wore at the beginning of the service, for a favorite bathrobe and slippers. Then she sat in a rocking chair in front of the altar, children gathered around her as she read the story of the Nativity. The eager youngsters and Amy's comfortable demeanor helped restore my holiday spirit.

After the service I asked if we could drive by the cemetery again to make sure the candles were still burning. They were. We could even see them from the highway as we approached. More candles had been added by Linda's friend, Susan. Linda's was the brightest spot in the cemetery on that Christmas Eve, but her grave still looked very cold and lonely. My emotion caught up with me as we walked away and Tina took my arm in reassuring, silent support.

THE NEW YEAR SAW Lamar and I off to Sanibel Island, Florida again with our friends the Bierks. This time we had rented a house and this time we stayed for the full month. Warm weather, walking on the beach, taking long bike rides and working on jigsaw puzzles was therapeutic.

When we returned we were prepared to return to some of our many avocations and activities. Lamar immersed himself in work for the community as chair of the Lakes and Dams Committee. Since he felt he still had some idle hours he started to work part-time at a home supply store. I resumed my active involvement with the NEA retired group and continued my part-time travel consultant job. I also started writing this book.

I signed Jared up for swimming lessons at the YMCA. As a frequent visitor to our lakefront home, he needed to be able to swim. Swim lessons were something that had been neglected the year before. Once a week for fourteen weeks, Tuesday afternoons were a time for us to be together. In June he stayed with us during the week for swimming lessons in the pool here. He learned to swim like a fish and also had a break from the pre-school setting, as wonderful as that setting was.

Spring brought the garden alive again. Since Lamar had kept everything watered the previous summer, the garden hadn't suffered too much. I added to my extensive hosta collection and Lamar and I made plans to expand the garden even more.

Dave seemed to be adjusting, too. He was cautiously resuming a social life. With the help of a friend, he finished decorating the family room and kitchen dining area. I helped him pick out some shrubbery for the side of the house, launching the re-landscaping project. Rick and Rachel came for Memorial Day weekend. Rick helped Dave remove the shutters on the outside of the house, sagging after thirty years while Rachel and I took Jared to Six Flags for the Missouri NEA day. While we waited in long, hot lines for the newest Scooby Doo ride, Rachel and I had a chance to reminisce, sharing memories of some of the good times as well as the bad.

Dave and Jared took a short vacation in Tennessee in June. In July they visited Rick and Rachel at their summer cottage in Wisconsin, something Linda had enjoyed both as a new bride and, later, as a new mother.

Mid-summer, I went to the NEA convention once more but without the anxiety of the year before, each day wondering what was happening at home. At the end of July, Lamar and I left for another trip, this time to Maine to visit Dave and Tina and then on to the Maritime Provinces. After two weeks exploring this beautiful area, we made a return stop in Maine, to join in the surprise early sixtieth birthday party for my brother that Tina and his sons had planned. My father was there, too, as an additional surprise – just shy of turning 90 himself.

The morning we left Maine we had one more mission – to distribute my mother's ashes (per her request) in beautiful Casco Bay. We had two urns. One urn contained my mother's ashes; the other contained the ashes of my brother's beloved black lab, Chowder. Chowder had loved the ocean as much as my mother.

It was a clear, bright, beautiful Maine morning. The sea was calm as we started off by boat towards the rocks out in the bay that the local seals call home. Tina took a picture of my nephew, Jon, and me, holding our respective urns. We are smiling broadly and look as if we might be going to a clambake which, of course, we weren't. But it wasn't a sad occasion. My mother was old and well past her "best if used by date," as she would say. She had had a full and rich life and her ashes were going to a place she loved. So were Chowder's.

The seals watched as we released the ashes, then slithered into the water, swimming to us with the curiosity that is their nature. The setting was spectacular.

My mother would have been pleased.

BECAUSE MY LIFE pathways lead me in different circles, I don't see too much of the teachers and students at Mason Ridge. I returned to the school in the fall to attend a special after-school session arranged by one of the counselors to help bring some closure to the kids. Debbie joined me for the first theater event of the season. We joined the other theater group teachers for dinner afterwards, including Jan. By request, Jan had made the reservation for one more person than we actually had. We saved that place – for Linda – and drank a toast to her.

On another occasion I joined Debbie's class on a field trip to St. Charles, Missouri's first state capitol. I returned again to collect some books that Linda had left behind. My first reaction was just to have them put in the library or a classroom. But someone insisted I might want to go through them first. I was glad I did. Among the books were books I had read to Linda as a child. I've set up a little library at home to share with Jared when he visits. He loves to see his mommy's scribbling that appears in some of the books.

This August, just before school started, all of us – Dave, Lamar, Jared and I – were invited back to Mason Ridge for another walkathon, arranged by one of the same girls who had organized the walkathon the previous year. This was Sami's community service *baht mitzvah* project. A late summer thundershower reduced the attendance, but Sami and her dad were wearing ponchos and doing laps in the rain, when we arrived. In spite of the uncooperative weather, the walkathon raised over $2500 to help fight cancer – just one small example of how Linda's legacy lives on.

YES, WE HAVE adjusted, each in our own way, each in our own time. Not a day goes by, however, when I don't think of Linda. Something triggers a memory or I look up at the clouds and wonder what she might be doing, if she knows how much I love her. I often think of her when I see a young family together, not people I know but total strangers, parents with young children enjoying their time together. If they could read my thoughts they would hear what I'm thinking.

Enjoy these precious times. They will pass all too quickly. Cherish them. Now.

Thoughts regarding *The Classroom is Bare . . .*

MOST OF US HAVE TEACHERS that we remember, some vividly, others less so. We remember because these teachers had an impact on our lives – they shaped what we did and who we became. As we graduated from high school, then college, some of us may have thought about writing a thank you note or dropping by to say, "Thanks, Mrs/Mr Jones or Smith or (you fill in the blank), you made a difference in my life."

If you are like most of us, however, you probably never followed through on that notion. And, if you did, you more than likely visited a college or high school teacher – certainly not a teacher from your elementary grades. Elementary teachers rarely get that kind of feedback.

Linda Favero did, however. She heard first-hand from her fifth graders and from former students, now in high school, whom she'd had as fifth graders. Granted, it took a devastating illness to generate the hundreds of notes and cards from students, parents and former students – and their parents.

The Classroom is Bare is the title of a poem written by Mara Lesser, a second grader, that was delivered to Linda in the hospital. Mara wasn't even one of Linda's students but a younger sibling of a fifth grader who shared her brother's concern for Mrs. Favero. The poem expresses how alone the children feel without their teacher. Just as any good teacher, "programs" their students to keep working without their immediate presence, the poem says that the children keep "working and working as hard as they should." And, when the teacher returns the classroom is not bare anymore.

Linda was not able to return to her classroom as her students had hoped but her classroom is not bare. It's full of the students whom she influenced, whose spark of imagination she captured, whose inspiration she encouraged. She taught her students far more than the lessons of the day. She taught them humor, and courage, and respect for one another. She taught all of us to make each day count.

Recently I received a copy of an essay from one of Linda's former fifth graders, Katelyn Whitfield, now a senior in high school, planning to become a teacher. Katelyn submitted the essay as part of her application for a scholarship awarded by the Parkway NEA to a student in each of the four Parkway high schools who plans to become a teacher. (Ironically, this scholarship was established when I was president of the local in the early 1980's.) Applicants were asked to write about an influential mentor. Katelyn concludes her essay by saying,

"Mrs. Favero impacted my life in a way no one had previous to her, and no one has since. She was an amazing person, full of color and passion. When people looked at her, they knew she was something special. In the classroom, she lit up the faces of her students. Every student wanted to please her. She made wanting to succeed desirable. I want my future students to feel that same way. I want kids to understand how important life is, and why it's vital to always be thankful for everything that comes your way. I will be sure to tell my students why I chose the profession I did, and how amazing of a person Mrs. Favero truly was. Hopefully, I can dramatically influence someone else's life, the way Linda Favero did for me."

Share Your Story

THE AUTHOR IS INTERESTED IN hearing from you about a teacher that made a difference in your life. What was it about that teacher that made him or her special to you? How did he or she make a difference in your life?

These anecdotes may be shared as the author speaks to groups about the impact of teachers on students lives.

Send your thoughts to Martha Karlovetz at Linmar Publications, PO Box 1222, Lake Sherwood, MO 63357; or e-mail: Linmarpub@aol.com

Credits and Acknowledgements

Page 36   Photo reprinted by permission, Picture Perfect
                 Studios, Manchester, MO

Pages 59-60   Title poem, *The Classroom is Bare,* reprinted
and   by permission, Herbert M. Lesser.
pages 209-210

Page 84   *My Hero,* reprinted by permission, Laura
                 Liberman

Page 198   Photo reprinted by permission, Wagner
                 Portrait Group, Bridgeton, MO

Page 200   Photo reprinted by permission, Sears Portrait
                 Studio, Chesterfield, MO

Page 211   *To Those I Love,* Isla Richardson, copyright
                 expired, Library of Congress

Page 213   *Let There Be Peace on Earth,* lyrics, copyright
                 1955 by Jan-Lee Music. Copyright renewed
                 1983. Used by permission; all rights reserved.

About the Author

MARTHA KARLOVETZ HAS TAUGHT AT the elementary, junior high and graduate levels. For nine years she served as president of the Missouri National Education Association (MNEA), advocating for educators through speeches and published columns.

Karlovetz is a recognized leader in public education in Missouri. She was appointed by Governor John Ashcroft and re-appointed by Governor Mel Carnahan to the Education Commission of the States. She helped draft the Outstanding Schools Act to ensure meaningful education reform in Missouri and worked to achieve its passage and implementation. Her name appears in the National Teachers' Hall of Fame.

Karlovetz is the editor of *When You Catch 'em, Parent-directed Activities for Young Children* and the author of *Teacher's Stuff, Reading and Language Activities for Teachers.*

She is proud that her daughter, Linda, chose to become a teacher.

Share
The Classroom is Bare
with a friend —

Do you know someone else who would enjoy reading this book?

To order additional copies, go to:
www.classroomisbare.com
or mail your order to Linmar Publications.

The Classroom is Bare, ISBN : 0-9741119-0-2, $15.95 each

Yes, please send me additional copies of *The Classroom is Bare*:

_____ *copies @ $15.95 each:*   _____

Sales tax: Missouri residents add
$1.00 sales tax each book: _____

Shipping: add $4.00 for the first book,
$1.00 for each additional book: _____

Total: _____

Name _____

Address _____

City_____ State _____ Zip _____

Phone _____

Checks should be made out to Linmar Publications. Mail to:
Linmar Publications, PO Box 1222, Lake Sherwood, MO 63357.

In memory of Linda Favero,

**The American Brain Tumor Association
has awarded a
$50,000 Translational Research Grant to:**

Radoslaw Zagozdzon, MD, PhD
Beth Israel Deaconess Medical Center
Boston, Massachusetts
July 2003

A FEW OF THE RESOURCES
AND SUPPORT SERVICES

FOR CANCER PATIENTS AND THEIR FAMILIES

American Brain Tumor Association
2720 River Road, Suite 146
Des Plaines, IL 60018
847-827-9910   FAX: 847-827-9918
1-800-886-2282
E-mail: info@abta.org
Internet address: www.abta.org

American Cancer Society
Internet address: www.cancer.org

Cancer Care, Inc.
1180 Avenue of the Americas
New York, NY 10036
212-302-2400
1-800-813-HOPE (1-800-813-4673)

Cancer Survivors Network
Sponsored by the American Cancer Society
1-877-333-HOPE (1-877-333-4673)
www.cancersurvivorsnetwork.org

Dow Corning Wright
Breast Implant Information Center
1-800-442-5442

Gillette Women's Cancer Connection
1-800-688-9777
www.gillettecancerconnect.org

National BMT (Bone Marrow Transplant) Link
29209 Northwestern Highway #624
Southfield, MI 48034
248-932-8483   1-800-LINK-BMT (1-800-546-5268)
comnet.org/NBMLINK

National Brain Tumor Foundation
414 Thirteenth Street, Suite 700
Oakland, CA 94612-2603
510-839-9777   FAX 510-839-9779
1-800-934-2873
www.braintumor.org

The National Cancer Institute
Cancer Information Service
Office of Cancer Communications
Bethesda, MD 20892
1-800-4-CANCER (1-800-422-6237)
www.NCI.NIH.gov

National Coalition for Cancer Survivorship
877-622-7937
E-mail: info@cansearch.org
Internet Address: www.cansearch.org

National Organization for Rare Disorders, INC. (NORD)
100 Route 37
P.O. Box 8923
New Fairfield, CT 06812-8923
203-746-6518
1-800-999-NORD (1-800-999-6673)
E-mail: orphan@nord-rdb.com
Internet Address: www.nord-rdb.com

National Ovarian Cancer Coalition
1451 West Cypress Creek Rd.
Ft. Lauderdale, FL 33309
954-351-9555 or 561-393-3220
E-mail: ovca@aol.com
Internet Address: www.ovarian.org

R.A.Bloch Cancer Foundation, Inc.
4410 Main Street
Kansas City, MO 64111
816-932-8453
1-800-433-0464 (Hotline)

The Susan B. Komen Breast Cancer Foundation
5005 LBJ Freeway, Suite 250
Dallas, TX 75244
972-855-1600   FAX: 972-855-1605
972-855-1601   1-800-I'M AWARE (1-800-462-9273)

Y-ME National Breast Cancer Hotline
212 W. Van Buren
Chicago, IL 60607
312-986-8228
1-800-221-2141